KU-251-993

TRUE GHOST STORIES

Kenneth Ireland

Hippo Books
Scholastic Publications Limited
London

Other titles by Kenneth Ireland available from Hippo:

Unsolved Mysteries
Treasure!

Scholastic Publications Ltd,
10 Earlham Street, London WC2H 9RX, UK

Scholastic Inc,
730 Broadway, New York, NY 10003, USA

Scholastic Tab Publications Ltd,
123 Newkirk Road, Richmond Hill,
Ontario L4C 3G5, Canada

Ashton Scholastic Pty Ltd,
PO Box 579, Gosford, New South Wales,
Australia

Ashton Scholastic Ltd,
165 Marua Road, Panmure, Auckland 6,
New Zealand

Copyright © Kenneth Ireland, 1989

Published by Scholastic Publications Limited, 1989

ISBN 0 590 76134 X

Made and printed by Cox & Wyman Ltd, Reading, Berks
Typeset in Plantin by AKM Associates (UK) Ltd., Southall, London

10 9 8 7 6 5 4 3 2 1

Contents

Introduction

Do you believe in ghosts? Anyone can say they've seen a ghost, but unless several people have seen or heard the same thing and are convinced of what they have seen, there is no real evidence at all.

But in every story in this collection a mysterious apparition or force has been witnessed by several people – sometimes whole crowds have experienced a supernatural occurrence – and no one has been able to give a satisfactory explanation for what they saw.

There are a number of theories which attempt to explain ghosts. One is that they are the spirits of the dead trapped on earth. Another is that they are apparitions which can be seen only by certain people as the result of telepathy – the passing of mental signals from one mind to another. Yet another theory is that where there has been a scene involving violent emotion, such as a murder, the surroundings somehow record the event – rather as a record or a tape

1

does – and then when conditions are right, the scene is played back.

Poltergeists might be different. These are forces which move things about. These might not be true ghosts at all, but the result of what is called psycho-kinetic energy – some mysterious force which is actually generated in somebody's mind – and usually that somebody has to be quite young.

So it is possible that ghosts might not really exist, although they may appear to be there to some people. On the other hand, some things don't seem to fit any of these theories – and when you have read the rest of this true collection of hauntings and things that go bump in the night, you can make up your own mind . . .

The Writing on the Wall

It was a pleasant house in a pleasant little town in the Bay of Fundy, Nova Scotia – Number 6, Princess Street, Amherst. In the house lived Daniel Teed and his wife, Olive, with their two children, William, aged five, and George, aged two. But because the house was large enough, also living there were Daniel Teed's brother, John, and Olive Teed's brother, William Cox – together with Olive's two sisters, Jean Cox, aged twenty-one, and Esther Cox, aged eighteen. Both William Cox and John Teed worked at the Amherst Shoe Factory, and so did Bob McNeal. In fact, until Esther Cox went out one evening with Bob McNeal, no one would have guessed the horrors which were to come.

Bob McNeal was tall, handsome, and regarded by all the Amherst girls as a great catch. But then on the night of 28th August, 1878, Esther Cox went out with him in a horse-drawn two-seater buggy which he had borrowed. Something unpleasant happened during

3

that evening, which ended with Bob McNeal threatening Esther with a gun. Then he changed his mind, drove her home – it was pouring with rain now – and dumped her at the gate of 6, Princess Street, before driving off.

The same night he left Amherst and was never heard of in the area again. In the meantime, Esther Cox, soaking wet from the rain, rushed into the house, went straight to bed, and cried herself to sleep. Her one evening with the local heart-throb had been a total disaster. Her sister, Jean, who shared the same bed, was kept awake every night for the next week as she continued to cry herself to sleep.

"For heaven's sake, Esther, pull yourself together!" said her sister in desperation. And that was the moment the amazing events began – slowly at first, then gradually building up as the force apparently gathered power.

Esther stopped sobbing, and sat upright in the bed. They both saw a movement under the bedclothes.

"It's a mouse!" screamed Esther, and jumped out of bed. Jean jumped out with her. They drew back the bedclothes and searched.

"There's no mouse!" snapped Jean. "We must have imagined it."

They returned to bed. But the following night . . .

"There is a mouse," whispered Esther. "Look – you can see it moving. It's in bed with us again!"

So cautiously they crept out of the bed, drew the covers back – and nothing. But underneath the bed they heard a rustling coming from a green cardboard box which was filled with bits of cloth for making patchwork.

"It must be in there," whispered Jean.

They pulled the box into the centre of the room,

gently, ready to catch the mouse and kill it. Then without any warning the cardboard box lifted itself into the air and fell back to the floor. As they watched, it did it again – and this time both girls screamed.

Daniel Teed hurried into the room from where he had been sleeping to find what the trouble was.

"That box – it suddenly jumped into the air by itself!" said Jean.

Daniel glanced at her suspiciously, for she was not the sort to become hysterical. He poked at the box, then emptied it completely, bit by bit. Its only contents were the pieces of cloth.

"There's nothing there – get back to bed," he ordered, and returned grumbling to his own room.

"What was wrong?" asked his wife, Olive, as he climbed back into bed.

"Nothing. Just a nightmare or something," he grunted, and they went back to sleep.

Unfortunately, it was no nightmare. It was just the beginning of what was to come. The following night, 6th September, they had all gone to bed when Jean fetched Daniel and his wife into their room. Esther seemed to be ill.

"Oh, my goodness. Look at her!" said Olive Teed.

Esther's body had begun to swell. When they pulled back the clothes they found she was swollen from her chest right down to her feet. They had never seen anything like this before. While they were worrying about what they ought to do, there was the sound of a thunder-clap in the room.

"The house has been struck by lightning!" shouted Olive.

Daniel went over to the window, drew back the curtains and looked out. There were no clouds in sight. "It can't have been," said Daniel. "It's a star-lit night."

"So what caused it?" asked Olive anxiously. At once there were three more thunder-claps – coming from beneath the bed where Esther was lying!

They decided to wait, since there was nothing they could do, until morning – and by then, Esther was perfectly normal.

"Now look, nobody's to mention what happened here last night to anybody – right?" said Daniel. "We don't want the neighbours to start thinking there's something strange about us, do we?"

"Besides, there's probably a perfectly ordinary explanation," put in Olive hopefully. "It's – it's just something that happened, that's all."

The family decided that she must be right, for nothing else in the least strange took place – until thirteen days later, the night of 19th September. Jean noticed that Esther had begun to swell up again, and this worried her. What happened then took her totally by surprise, and she screamed.

Olive came in, wearing her night clothes.

"The bedclothes just leapt off the bed!" Jean said, trembling.

Olive glanced at the bed. The only covering left was the sheet on which the girls were lying.

"We've had enough of this nonsense," she said, and put the clothes back on the bed. "Now there'll be no more of it, do you hear? Pretending the bedclothes moved by themselves indeed! Oh my God!"

The bedclothes flew off into a corner of the room. This time Esther's pillow flung itself out from underneath her head and hit John Teed in the face as he and the rest of the inhabitants of the house came in to see what was causing the fuss.

"I've got a headache," whimpered Esther.

"William, go and fetch some cold water to bathe her forehead," ordered Olive. "That might help."

Even before he had returned with a pan of water and a cloth, though, there was a succession of noises like thunder coming from beneath the bed. At once Esther lost the swelling and returned to normal, and the noises stopped.

"Good morning, Daniel," greeted Dr Carritte the following morning at his surgery. "You look worried."

"It's not me, it's my sister-in-law, Esther," said Daniel Teed.

"So what's wrong with her?" asked the doctor. Daniel explained, rather hesitantly.

"Rubbish, man!" retorted Dr Carritte. "You haven't been drinking, have you?"

"Dr Carritte, we're Wesleyan Methodists, as you know," returned Daniel. "Do you think I'm making this up?"

The doctor considered carefully. "All right. If Esther's body starts to swell again, you can send for me. Because that at least would be a medical matter. But flying bedclothes and mysterious claps of thunder – well, you can't expect me to believe that, can you?"

Dr Carritte, however, soon had to believe it. About ten o'clock that same night he was sent for urgently. Esther had begun to swell. He arrived with his bag and was taken up to the girls' bedroom to see his patient. Since the whole household were now involved in the affair one way or another, they all trooped in behind him.

Before the doctor began his examination, the pillow under Esther's head moved away from the bed by itself then returned to its place. While the doctor watched in astonishment, it moved out a second time. John Teed rushed forwards and grabbed hold of it now, but whatever force was moving the pillow was too strong for him, and he couldn't prevent it from returning to underneath Esther's head. Then came a loud thunder-clap. Then the bedclothes flew off.

"Believe it now, do you?" demanded Daniel Teed grimly.

They stood back from the bed, wondering what was going to happen next. There was a feeling in the room which Dr Carritte couldn't place, as if something horrible was about to happen. They waited.

The wall behind the bed was made of plaster. Then suddenly there was a movement in the plaster, as if something was about to burst out at them. As they drew back, further away from it, a letter appeared, an E. Then an S. Then more. It was as if they were being cut into the wall by an invisible knife. Then the entire message appeared, cut into the wall: *ESTHER COX YOU ARE MINE TO KILL*

Dr Carritte and the entire household apart from Esther, who seemed to be unconscious, left the room in a hurry. The rest of the family were sent away while Dr Carritte discussed what was best to do now with Mr and Mrs Teed, standing clear of the doorway and against the wall outside.

A piece of plaster detached itself from the wall of the bedroom and landed at Dr Carritte's feet. If the doctor had not been absolutely convinced before then, he certainly was now. The only way that plaster could have landed where it did was by flying through the air and then turning a corner by itself before it landed!

Then the loud pounding noises started again,

shaking the bedroom and all its contents, and this time lasted for two hours before coming to a stop.

Dr Carritte wrote his account of the matter later on, and his opinion was that in the house was certainly an invisible power "of a very low order of intelligence" and "a demonical type". He considered that its presence had to be directly connected with what he called Esther's "nervous excitation".

But that was later on. In the meantime, he left the house, since the disturbance had now come to an end. The next morning Esther got up and helped with the housework as usual, just as if nothing had happened. The doctor called again.

"And how do you feel this morning?" he asked. "The swelling has completely gone, I see."

"I feel quite all right, thank you, doctor," replied Esther, "except that I jump now at any sudden noise. But then, I suppose that's to be expected, isn't it?"

"You've had no further trouble, then?"

"Well – I've just been down into the cellar with a pan of milk and somebody down there threw a plank at me."

"Show me," said the doctor, so Esther led him to the cellar steps.

He went down, looked all round, and found nothing unusual. "Come down and show me," he called. So Esther descended the cellar steps as well.

As soon as she was standing alongside him at the foot of the steps a pile of potatoes flew at them, apparently aiming themselves at their heads! They both hurried up the cellar steps and closed the door behind them.

"I am convinced," said Dr Carritte to Daniel and Olive Teed, "of one thing – somehow the force, whatever it is, is coming from her. So what I intend to do now is return this evening, just before she goes to bed, and give her an injection to calm her down. Hopefully, that will cure whatever is wrong."

"You mean it's all Esther's fault, then?" asked Olive anxiously.

"No. But I think that somehow she is the cause, without knowing it. If we cure her, we cure the whole business, I'm pretty sure of that."

That evening, he filled the hypodermic syringe. "This won't hurt," he assured her. "Just bare your arm for me, will you? There. Now just get into bed, and everything will be all right." He hoped that he sounded convincing.

He glanced up at the message cut into the plaster of the bedroom wall. There was no mistaking the genuineness of that. It had happened while he had been watching, quite out of the reach of anyone in the room at the time. This time, before he had even left the room, having made sure that Esther was safely in bed, loud bangs were coming from the girls' bed, louder than ever before. Then the sounds moved. Now they appeared to be coming from somewhere in the roof of the house instead. He stared at the ceiling now.

There just had to be an explanation! It just had to be something happening outside the house which was causing this astonishing banging noise. So he went out of the house and looked up at the roof. There was absolutely nothing visible anywhere on the roof, but from outside it sounded exactly as if somebody was pounding it with a sledgehammer. But no damage was being done, apparently. He could still hear the banging going on as he walked home.

A few nights later, there were two clergymen at the door. One was the Wesleyan minister, Mr Temple.

"I think you know the Baptist minister, the Reverend Clay?" he said to Daniel.

"Of course."

Daniel knew why they had come. The extremely loud noises coming from the house were beginning to disturb the neighbours, and the affair could no longer be kept quiet.

"Come in if you must." Daniel led them upstairs. They waited a short while, and experienced the noises for themselves.

"Would you mind if we called in Dr Tupper?" asked Mr Temple.

Daniel knew of Dr Nathan Tupper. He was the only other church minister in the town of Amherst. Rather grudgingly, he agreed. If this was all the work of the devil, at least three clergymen ought to be able to put a stop to it.

Dr Tupper was sceptical, to say the least. After the performance, they all gathered downstairs in the house.

"Gentlemen," said Dr Tupper, "what I say is that Esther Cox is a fraud. She is causing these disturbances herself, deliberately."

"But how can she be doing that? You saw for herself, she didn't move, she lay there in the bed."

"In that case, somehow she is mesmerizing people into believing that these things are happening. She's just using some sort of hypnotism on everybody, and we're falling for it. I tell you what I think is the best course of treatment," he added. "Get a raw-hide whip and drive the devil out of her by using it on her. That's what I advise!"

"Thank you for your help," said Daniel Teed bitterly.

But even without the use of a raw-hide whip, all the

disturbances came to an end. Esther Cox caught diphtheria. This was often a deadly disease, for diphtheria causes a membrane to grow across the throat, and if the treatment is not successful the patient is suffocated by it. If the treatment is begun too late, the patient dies anyway, because of the infection spreading through the body.

Dr Carritte managed to save her life, however, and as soon as she was well enough she was sent to stay with another married sister, Mrs Snowdon, at Sackville, ten miles away, for a couple of weeks, so that she could fully recover.

It was now January, 1879. "Welcome home, Esther," said Olive Teed. "Let me show you your new bedroom."

"Why aren't I having my old one?" asked Esther.

"So the power won't follow you, we hope," said Olive brightly.

But it did. When Jean and Esther were in their bed in their new bedroom, a lighted match fell from the ceiling on to the bed. Jean jumped out of bed and managed to extinguish it, but within the next ten minutes eight more lighted matches fell, apparently from nowhere, on to the bed, and had to be extinguished as well.

By now Jean was beginning to become suspicious. Objects flying about were one thing, writing appeared on the wall by itself similarly – but Esther could have thrown the lighted matches up to the ceiling herself. Then three days later a fire started in the cellar. They managed to put it out with buckets of water.

"Where was Esther at the time?" asked Jean grimly.

"She was in the dining room," replied Olive. "She never left it. Why do you ask?"

"I just wondered," said Jean casually.

During the next week there were more rappings, bangings, thunder-claps – and more fires mysteriously started. While all of these happenings were quite outside the experience of anyone living in the town of Amherst, the neighbours were sympathetic. In particular was John White sympathetic.

"Now look here," he told Daniel and Olive, "I know what trouble you've been having. How would it suit if I took Esther off your hands and had her live round at my place? My wife would welcome a little housework being done, to help her out, and that would be payment enough."

Esther was agreeable. "I'm sure it won't follow me there!" she said.

She was wrong, but it took three weeks before anything happened. A scrubbing brush flew from her hand, hit the ceiling and struck Esther on the head as it returned to earth. At once the kindly John White took her to work with him instead. That was no problem, for John White owned a restaurant in the town. The problem was that while she was working in the restaurant customers and staff suddenly found that doors would open by themselves, with no one near them; furniture would move about; and on one occasion Dr Carritte had to be called to the restaurant because a boy sitting at one of the tables for some reason had his penknife in his hand – it left his hand, flew through the air and stabbed itself into Esther's back. The power had obviously found her again!

By now, more help was offered to try to separate Esther from whatever was the cause of the trouble. A Captain James Beck and his wife invited her to stay with them at St John's, New Brunswick, about 100 miles away from Amherst. They had read about Esther Cox's strange case in the newspapers. Esther stayed with them for three weeks, then for the next eight weeks was invited to live with the Van Ambergh family on a farm close to Amherst.

All was peaceful. All seemed to be over. Just a brief newspaper paragraph announced that she had now returned home to the Teeds' house at 6, Princess Street, Amherst. Then there was a new arrival on the scene.

"I'm Walter Hubbell," he announced, "and I was just wondering if you could put me up for a while – as a paying guest, so to speak."

"You're not a newspaper reporter, are you?" asked Mrs Teed doubtfully.

Walter Hubbell laughed. "No I'm not, ma'am. I'm an actor. I'm resting at the moment, of course, but I can pay my way if you have room in the house."

What the Teeds did not know at the time was that Walter Hubbell was an out-of-work actor who from the stories in the newspaper saw a chance to make some money out of the curious situation in Amherst. That was the real reason for his arrival. First, though, he had to convince himself that the newspaper stories were true. So he made sure that wherever Esther was in the house, he was never far away.

He was soon convinced. Esther was dusting at one end of the parlour. Fifteen feet away at the far end of the room a glass paper-weight stood on a table. The paper-weight flew by itself through the air towards her.

During the next few days, while Esther was in the room, a china sugar bowl disappeared – vanished while he watched. Ten minutes later it reappeared when it fell from the ceiling and smashed itself on the floor. An inkstand and two bottles hurtled through the air in his direction, and a fire started, apparently by itself. He was certainly convinced by now, and put his proposition to the Teeds.

"I don't know that it would be right," said Daniel doubtfully.

"Look, you might as well make some money out of it as not. Don't you think so, Mrs Teed?" he asked, turning to her. "All the suffering and damage you've been through – you might as well raise some cash out of it to pay for it, wouldn't you say?"

So he hired a hall in the town, sold tickets, and put Esther Cox on stage to demonstrate her "powers". He was certain he was about to make a fortune out of the unfortunate girl. What he failed to understand was that Esther did not, apparently, set out to make these strange things happen. The show was a complete flop. In front of an audience she could make absolutely nothing happen at all, and far from making a fortune the audience demanded their money back.

Walter Hubbell left the town immediately. (Later he did make a great deal of money by writing a totally exaggerated book about Esther Cox.)

But it was not only Walter Hubbell who had had enough by now. So had the Teed family, and the disastrous public performance was the last straw! Apart from the unwelcome publicity which they had received, many of the walls and doors of their house had been damaged in the course of the "happenings", much of the furniture and most of the crockery in the house had been smashed – so they moved out, and never lived in the house again.

"But what about me?" asked Esther. "What am I going to do?"

"You needn't worry about that," said her sister kindly. "That's been all fixed up. You're going to work at the Arthur Davison farm, near the Van Amberghs'. It's not far away, just a few miles. Mr Davison would like you to help around the house, that's all."

So to the Arthur Davisons' Esther went. It was a worse disaster this time, but entirely Esther Cox's own fault. Some clothes were found to be missing from the house, and then they were discovered in a barn. Esther was suspected of stealing them, but before anything could be done, the barn in which they had been found mysteriously burned down. Esther was convicted of arson, and sentenced to four months in prison.

Shortly after coming out of prison, she married. All the troubles came to an end, and she died in 1912, never bothered by those strange forces again.

So what is the truth? Although the events took place more than a century ago, they are well-documented, and even though science had not made the enormous strides which it has made since, the people who witnessed or were involved in the happenings were not gullible or ignorant.

In 1907 Hereward Carrington, a psychical researcher, began an investigation. In particular he interviewed people who had been there at the time. By now Dr Carritte was dead, Jean Cox, William Cox and John Teed had all left the area and couldn't be contacted, but Daniel and Olive Teed were willing to talk.

Olive Teed said that while Walter Hubbell's book "dramatized and embellished the truth", it was basically accurate. In particular, she told Hereward

Carrington, "a terrible reality" was the writing which appeared on the wall. There had been no possibility of a fake about that. They had all been terrified when that had happened.

He visited Arthur Davison, and what Davison told him came rather as a surprise. There was no doubt that Esther had stolen some clothes, and then had set fire to the barn deliberately when she was found out – no doubt trying to pretend that it was "the force" at work again. But what he also said of Esther Cox was that "a better girl we never had" – until the theft and the fire – and he also added that she was such a good worker that they put up with articles in the house throwing themselves about every now and then, and other curious happenings like Esther's body swelling up when she seemed to be either unconscious or asleep!

Then Carrington went to Massachusetts, where Esther was now living as a married woman. The "power" had not visited her since, but she was very reluctant to talk about it in case it came back!

Carrington then enquired of her various other employers to get their opinion about Esther. She was regarded as "respectable, honest and reliable, and not at all of an imaginative turn of mind". In fact, respectable, hard-working, but not very bright!

The final investigation took place eight years after Esther had died, in 1920. Dr Walter Price also looked into the affair. His conclusion was that Esther might have had a split personality. He also believed that she "helped out" some of the later happenings in this strange case – but not any of those at the beginning.

Once conclusion is certain – at the beginning,

and for some considerable time, there was a poltergeist, coming either from Esther Cox or from her surroundings, and there was no way in which anyone could stop it. The evidence for that is quite beyond all dispute – or understanding.

The Ghosts of the Rambling House

It was broad daylight on a warm summer's evening. Along the path which bordered the large rectory garden and ran parallel to the road beyond the gate walked a nun in her black robes, her head bowed. She took no notice of the three girls, Ethel, Freda and Mavel Bull, as they ran in through the gate. They had just returned home from a garden party.

The girls stopped, wondering what they ought to do.

"I think perhaps one of us should go and fetch Dodie," one said. Dodie was another sister, who had stayed at home.

"What's wrong?" asked Dodie.

"Come quickly, there's a nun on the path."

"So? Have you asked her what she wants?"

"Well – no. But we think you ought to come and see."

So Dodie came out of the house to investigate. She knew why her sisters were worried, but when she saw their visitor she realized they had no reason to be scared at all. This was a real nun, there was no doubt about that. She was just a woman walking along the path round their garden, no doubt come to see the rector on some church matter.

Her three sisters remained together now, just in case, but Dodie walked briskly towards the nun.

"Can I help you?" she asked.

The nun stopped, looked towards all four of them – and immediately vanished. The date was 28th July, 1901, and all four of the rector's daughters who were in the garden that evening had no doubt of what they had seen.

The rectory was in the village of Borley in Suffolk, and it had a famous reputation. The ugly, large, rambling house was built in 1863 for the Reverend Henry Bull, the new rector of Borley. It had not always been so rambling, but as Henry Bull's family increased in size he had added to it. But the troubles began almost as soon as they had moved into the new house. It started with the sound of footsteps, and then they heard tappings in the walls, and then even mysterious voices which appeared to be answering each other.

Before long the situation had grown worse. One of the rector's children was woken one night by a slap across the face – and no one was there. Another woke up one night to find a man in old-fashioned clothes standing by her bed. He just vanished. Then the ghostly nun appeared. Whatever else, she invariably appeared every 28th July. Even Borley church was affected, for sometimes chanting was heard coming from it at night when the church was deserted.

Mr and Mrs Bull went to great lengths to keep the stories of the hauntings within the family. They even instructed the children never to even talk about ghosts, not even inside the house. When the rector and his wife invited people to visit them, it was only to lunch or tea – never dinner in the evenings, because of what they might see.

In fact, Henry Bull even had a window in the house bricked up so that the ghostly nun, who often appeared on the pathway outside, was no longer able to peer in through the window while the family were eating.

Henry Bull was the rector of Borley for thirty years, until he died in 1892, and during that time the noises and apparitions hardly ever ceased, and most of the local people kept well away from the rectory. Various suggestions were made to explain the curious happenings. One was that the house was haunted by the spirits of a monk and a nun who centuries before had eloped from Bures, about eight miles away. Since it was forbidden for monks and nuns to marry, when they had been caught the monk had been hanged and the nun had been bricked up alive. That was an unlikely explanation. There is no evidence that anything of the sort ever happened. In addition, it is known that if a priest or a monk centuries ago committed a crime punishable by death – and marrying was not one of those crimes – he would have been suspended in a cage without food or water until he starved himself to death!

When Henry Bull died, the new rector of Borley was his son, the Reverend Henry Foyster Bull, who of course had been brought up in the house. To avoid confusion, the new rector was known as Harry Bull, and he lived in the rectory until he died in 1927.

Unlike his father, he made no attempt to disguise what was going on in his house. He even had a summer house erected facing the path which the family called the Nun's Walk, so he could watch the ghostly nun going by! He quite enjoyed having the ghosts in his house, and would often mention to his congregation in church such things as, "The nun was busy again last night!"

But during his thirty-five years as rector, the power seemed to be increasing. Other happenings were queer padding noises in the house, the sound of crockery being smashed, footsteps, and the appearance of a man's shape, in addition to everything else. But there was nothing especially frightening yet . . . the ghosts were there, and that was all there was to it!

Even Mr and Mrs Cooper, who lived in the nearby cottage and were employed by the Bull family, were not scared. They saw the nun and experienced those other inexplicable happenings many times. It didn't worry them – except that Mr Cooper also discovered one moonlit night a coach and horses driving without a sound across the yard outside his bedroom window. It was complete, even to the two lamps being lit, with somebody sitting on the driving box, and the trappings shining in the moonlight. It drove across his yard, out of the rectory gate, across the road, and then disappeared as it went towards the church. What no one knew at the time, or for years later, was that there had once been an old road which ran exactly along the path which the phantom coach had taken, before the houses were built.

However, after the Reverend Harry Bull died in 1927, it took a long time to find anyone who was willing to become the new rector of Borley, because of its reputation. In fact, the rectory remained empty for sixteen months, until the Reverend Eric Smith and his wife moved into the large house. They had just returned from India, and had heard nothing about what was likely to be in store for them.

They lasted for just nine months. What they found was that in addition to everything else, now keys, vases and other objects in the house suddenly flew through the air for no reason. In the garden pebbles would suddenly take off from the ground and throw themselves at people who were passing. The cook complained to the new rector that although every evening she locked the kitchen door, every morning it would be standing open and unlocked. Mysterious lights began to appear at the rectory windows, and on occasions Mrs Smith would be left shrieking with fright at what was going on around her!

In desperation, the Smiths left the house in July, 1929. A poltergeist now seemed to have appeared on the scene in addition to the usual activities!

It took until October of that year before another rector could be found who was willing to risk living in the house, but eventually the Bull family persuaded a cousin, the Reverend Lionel Foyster, to take it over. He moved in with his wife, Marianne, and their two-year-old adopted daughter.

Now the hauntings not only continued, but something worse was added. Writing began to appear on scraps of paper and on the walls and the wallpaper. Each time the message was the same: *Marianne get help*.

What was more, now a voice began to be heard, calling Marianne Foyster's name. And before long she found herself being attacked inside the house by some completely invisible force!

Doors locked and unlocked themselves, bells rang, strange smells became apparent, there were outbreaks of fire without any obvious cause, bottles appeared out of thin air and then disappeared again – and it was not only the rector and his wife who were experiencing these things, for members of his family who were visiting, friends, even complete strangers who had called at the house discovered them. It was surprising that the Foysters stuck it out for five years, until 1935.

When they left, the house was never lived in again. The new rector, the Reverend Alfred Henning, was in charge of both Borley and Liston – and preferred to live at Liston Rectory instead!

But someone did move in, but not to live there: Harry Price, the most famous ghost-hunter in Britain, and founder of the National Laboratory for Psychical Research. He knew all the tricks which could be used to create "ghosts", and had exposed many frauds who had pretended to be "mediums".

Harry Price had been to the house before. At one time, in desperation, the Reverend Eric Smith had written to the *Daily Mirror* asking for help, and the editor had called him in to investigate. It had left him baffled at the time – except he did discover something new. When he asked the force to ring one of the house bells for him, it rang!

But now he had the chance to investigate properly. He rented the rectory for a year from May, 1937, then advertised in *The Times* newspaper for volunteers to assist him. He wanted educated people who would record under scientific conditions any inexplicable happenings which might take place, and he selected forty-eight people for his team – doctors, engineers, scientists, and others whom he thought unlikely to see things which weren't really there! Every effort was made to make sure there was no fraud involved, or any inaccurate observations.

What he and his team found were sudden drops of temperature for no apparent reason, smells like incense burning appearing from nowhere, tablets of soap thrown across rooms, stones being thrown about, and books moving entirely by themselves, items appearing and then disappearing, and patches of light becoming visible and then going. Harry Price used the rector's study as his office. One day, alone in that room with the door closed, he heard the key turn in the lock. The door was still closed, with the key on the inside, he found when he turned round, but now the door was locked. Whatever had locked that door must have been in the study with him, although no one was to be seen.

It was decided that the place really was haunted, and that there were spirits, probably evil, in the house. A decision was made to hold an exorcism. That was performed by a monk. While the monk was holding the service of exorcism, he was hit by flying pebbles. Obviously, exorcism was not going to work!

Later on, after Henry Price's death, it was suggested that Price himself was a fraud. If so, then his entire team of helpers were frauds as well, and so were all the members of the Bull family, the Foysters, the Smiths – and most of the population of the village of Borley.

The Church authorities now decided to sell the notorious rectory, and it was bought by a Captain W.H. Gregson. Since it was no longer a rectory, he changed the name of the house to Borley Priory. A change of name had no real effect, however. In fact, the house burned down at midnight on 27th February, 1939.

Captain Gregson was not at home at the time, and the house was empty, but many local people gathered as soon as the flames became visible. Several of them claimed to have seen the figure of a young girl at an upstairs window as the flames rose, but no body was found in the ruins afterwards. Many actually saw the figure of a nun leaving the house during the fire – but there were no nuns in the village of Borley.

But the end of the house did not end the curious happenings, for even though the house was no longer there, the ruins remained.

In 1939 the Second World War began. In every town and village local people were appointed to be Air Raid Wardens. Several times during the war the Air Raid Wardens were called out to the ruined house because there were lights shining from the windows. Except there could not have been any lights, because the house was a total ruin.

During the Second World War, too, the ruins were excavated. A medium, Helen Glanville, announced that she had discovered that the ghostly nun of Borley had been someone called Marie Lairre, who left her convent in Le Havre, France, to marry a member of the Waldegrave family living at Borley Place. Her husband strangled her in May, 1667, on the exact spot where the rectory was later built.

So in 1943 excavations began to see if what the medium had said could possibly be true. Four feet under the foundations were found human bones, including part of a woman's jaw-bone. They *could* have been the remains of the nun, or equally the remains might have been all that was left of a victim of the plague. No one can be sure.

What is sure is that the discovery of the bones did not entirely bring the happenings to an end. Another investigation took place in 1961. While that was going on, cameras, torches, even car headlights, all failed to work for no apparent reason. Other investigations were made, using infra-red cameras, walkie-talkies and sound recording equipment, some recording "happenings" and others not.

After the fire, the hauntings moved across to the cottage on the edge of the site and over the road to the church. At the cottage, for instance, there have been inexplicable loud noises, the shapes of people have been seen, voices have been heard, items have appeared and disappeared – and even a phantom cat has appeared a few times!

Even more curious, Borley was not the only rectory in that area to be haunted. Only a few miles away lies the village of Polstead. In 1978 the new rector of Polstead, the Reverend Foster, moved in with his wife and son. Five nights after moving in, Mrs Foster woke at about three o'clock in the morning to find the walls of the bedroom changing from being freshly-painted to looking like damp, peeling old wallpaper. Then she heard a child scream as if it was being strangled.

They left. The people of Polstead were not entirely surprised. The house had been known to have been haunted since at least 1795, and even in modern times a procession of monks had been seen crossing the road outside – except that their feet were several feet above the level of the road.

The Bishop, hearing about these hauntings at Polstead for the first time, asked the wife of the previous rector if she had experienced anything while they had been living there. Her answer was that they had grown used to hearing footsteps going upstairs when nobody was there, so took no notice of them!

So what is the truth about Borley Rectory? There have been so many strange, impossible and sometimes frightening occurrences happening there over the years, witnessed by so many independent unbiased and sensible people, some of whom have done all that was possible to find a logical explanation – that there is only one answer. And you know what it is!

The Ghost at the Moment of Death

Vice Admiral Sir George Tryon, Commander of the British fleet in the Mediterranean, made a terrible and inexplicable mistake. It was terrible because of the number of deaths which resulted, and inexplicable because Sir George Tryon was a highly experienced Admiral. It almost seemed as if his mind was somewhere else, later reports stated. Whatever the real cause, the outcome was a disaster.

The date was 22nd June, 1893. The Mediterranean fleet at the time consisted of eight battleships and five cruisers. They were all steam-driven, and were on manoeuvres off the coast of Tripoli. The Admiral's plan was that the fleet should first steam ahead in two columns, parallel to each other, in "line ahead". His flagship, *HMS Victoria*, would lead one of the columns, and *HMS Camperdown* was to lead the other.

"The columns are to remain six cable-lengths from each other," ordered Sir George.

A cable-length is 200 yards, or just short of 183 metres.

"When I give the command, the columns are to turn inwards towards each other, and then reverse course," Sir George announced.

"Excuse me, Sir," said an officer on the bridge of the flagship.

"What is it?" asked the Admiral.

"Might I suggest that six cable-lengths might be too small a distance? Could I suggest a distance of eight cable-lengths instead?"

Sir George considered. "Very well. Make the distance eight cable-lengths."

That would make the total distance between the two columns not far short of a mile. It would be much safer with that much space between them.

Then within minutes Sir George suddenly changed his mind. "Make a signal that the columns are to remain at six cable-lengths, as I originally commanded," instructed the Admiral.

His face looked blank at the time and his eyes were strangely dull as he made this correction to his orders, according to the evidence given at the Naval enquiry afterwards. His face still had the same expression when he shortly ordered the turn to begin.

Soon the ships at the head of the columns, the *Victoria* and the *Camperdown*, were heading towards each other on a collision course, at a combined speed of eighteen knots. Sir George, however, gave no orders to correct this.

"Sir," one of the officers on the bridge of the flagship said urgently, "it is essential that you give an order to change our course."

There was no answer. It was as if the Admiral had either not heard him, or not understood. Then, just at

30

the last moment, he seemed to wake himself up and order the engines to go full astern.

In a large ship, it takes time for a turn to be made or for the propellers, going in reverse, to slow a ship down and bring it to a halt. Admiral Sir George Tryon had given the order too late, and the *Victoria* and the *Camperdown* headed towards the inevitable collison.

Another officer ordered the bugler to sound "All hands on deck!", just as the *Camperdown* ran into the flagship about twenty metres behind the bows. The impact carried *HMS Camperdown* right through the iron-clad side of *HMS Victoria*.

Water immediately began to pour into the flagship. It was still possible that the ship's pumps could have coped even with that volume of sea water, if the Admiral had not at once given another order. He shouted to the Captain of *HMS Camperdown*.

"Go astern with both engines!"

"Sir, if we do that –" the Captain began to shout back.

"Follow your orders!" shouted Sir George.

The Captain had to obey the Admiral's order, and the *Camperdown* began to pull itself backwards out of the side of the *Victoria*. The enormous gash which was now exposed caused the flagship to be immediately and completely swamped, and as the water entered everything was swept before it. Men were caught below decks in the flooding compartments, not yet having had time to get on deck in answer to the bugle-call.

Six hundred men managed to escape by jumping from the ship into the Mediterranean. But many of these were killed either by being cut to pieces on the propellers, which were still turning, or were sucked down with *HMS Victoria* as it sank quickly to the bottom. 358 men died. One of those who drowned was Vice Admiral Sir George Tryon, who stayed on the bridge of his ship as it sank.

Meanwhile, at Eaton Place in Belgravia, London, Lady Tryon was having an "at home", and had invited many of London's fashionable society to the house where she and Sir George lived. She was chatting to some of her guests when she noticed that some of the others in the room had fallen silent and were drawing aside to let somebody pass by. Suddenly she screamed and the teacup fell from her hand. There was now total silence in the room.

In the full-dress uniform of a Vice Admiral, Sir George had walked down the curved staircase, then crossed the room full of guests, opened a door and passed through into the room beyond. One of the guests ran forward, opened the door again and looked inside the room into which Sir George had just walked. It was empty. It had to be – everyone present knew that Sir George could not have been there, because at the time he was on board his flagship in the Mediterranean.

Only later were the facts discovered: Sir George Tryon had drowned at almost the same time as a roomful of people had seen him in London, hundreds of miles away.

It has occasionally happened that people have been seen in some other place at the moment they have died, but almost invariably by only one person at a time. The apparition of Sir George Tryon was clearly visible, as if he were really present with them, by a crowd of people, all at the same time. And at that moment they were all totally unaware of the disaster which had occurred at sea.

Mrs Goddard's Coffin

Suppose that from within her coffin a dead woman could control events which take place around her. That is one possible explanation for this extraordinary story, but there is no way of knowing if it could be true.

Oistins, in Barbados, lies part-way between Worthing and South Point. This is the scene of a mystery which has never been solved, nor is it ever likely to be. There just is no logical explanation, unless you accept that some supernatural force was at work. Among those who have at various times tried to find a solution to the mystery have been Lord Combermere, who was the Governor of Barbados at the time, and Sir Arthur Conan Doyle, the creator of the fictional detective, Sherlock Holmes.

There is no dispute about the facts. They are clear and well-documented. But as for *how* it happened, no one knows . . .

Mr and Mrs Thomas Chase were sugar-planters in

Barbados. Their plantation was worked by slaves, like all the others on the island. In the cliffs above Oistins Bay lay a rock and stone tomb, sealed with a slab of marble and it is still there to this day. Mr and Mrs Chase acquired the tomb from the Goddard family in 1808. Inside was just one wooden coffin, containing the body of Mrs Thomasina Goddard.

In the nineteenth century families were large, and it was not at all certain that all of the children would live to become adults. So it was in the case of the Chase family. Within a year of taking over the tomb it was opened twice, for the burial of two of their children, Mary Ann and Dorcas. Their bodies were placed in lead coffins, and each time the marble slab was unsealed from the entrance to the tomb, and each time the slab was sealed up again immediately after the funeral. Stone masons had to be called in each time to break the seal and then to cement the marble slab back into place.

Four years after they had taken over the tomb, in 1812, Thomas Chase also died. Eight men carried his lead coffin to the tomb, the tomb was opened – and then came the first horrified surprise. Mrs Goddard's coffin was still in its right place, but the lead coffins of the two small children were standing on end against the wall.

The children's coffins were returned to where they should have been, then the coffin of Mr Chase was laid next to them. Then the stone masons recemented the marble slab across the entrance.

Sir Arthur Conan Doyle, when he investigated the story many years later, came to the conclusion that for some reason Thomas Chase had committed suicide instead of dying a natural death, but this has never been proved. But so far, it appeared that somebody had somehow managed to break into the tomb and disturb its contents. But since there was no other way in or out except by unsealing the marble slab, moving it, then afterwards sealing it up again, this was unlikely.

Four years later the tomb had to be opened again, this time to bury a relative. The cement seals were intact, nothing was disturbed on the outside – but inside, while Mrs Goddard's coffin remained undisturbed, all the other three coffins were scattered around the floor instead of being where they had been carefully placed.

Again the tomb had to be put into its right order, Thomas Chase's heavy coffin had to be man-handled back into position, and the new burial then took place. Two months later in the same year there had to be yet another funeral, and this time it was found that all four coffins had been moved, but still not Mrs Goddard's!

It was three years after that, in 1819, that the next family funeral took place. This time every coffin had been moved, they were scattered all round the floor of the tomb – except, again, that containing the remains of Mrs Thomasina Goddard.

Earth tremors were suspected of causing the disturbance of the coffins – except there had not been any. And even if there had been an earth tremor which nobody had noticed, Mrs Goddard's coffin would have been the one that should have moved, since it was the only coffin made of wood.

Flooding was considered – water entering and making the coffins float about, but this was impossible, too. Certainly Thomas Chase's coffin would not have floated, while Mrs Goddard's wooden one might have. But in any case there were no signs of water anywhere in the tomb, and if water had entered it should have left stains or water-marks at least. Also neither earth tremors nor a flood would have been likely to have left one of the least heavy coffins in the tomb untouched.

Interference by some of the islanders was a possibility, but not a very likely one. The islanders of Barbados were very superstitious about all burial grounds and other sacred places and also there was only one way in or out of the tomb, and the cement seals had never been disturbed between burials.

Just in case there was another way in, the walls and ceilings were checked meticulously. But these were of stone or solid rock, and no faults or cracks could be found anywhere.

The Governor of Barbados, Lord Combermere, had been invited to the funeral of 1819. When to his horror he saw the state of the tomb, he personally supervised the replacement of the coffins into some sort of order. He had the six coffins laid in a neat line, with the three smaller ones resting on top of those which contained the remains of adults.

And then he sprinkled a layer of fine sand all round the coffins and all over the floor. Sand would leave marks should anyone walk on it or anything be moved, and if the next time the tomb was opened there were marks in the sand, then that should provide a clue as to what was really taking place in there.

In addition to that, when the marble slab was returned to its position to block off the entrance, not only did Lord Combermere make absolutely certain that the masons had cemented it in properly, but he added his own seal across the joint. If anyone should try to break in now, the seal would be broken beyond repair.

The following year on 18th April, 1820, Lord Combermere ordered the tomb to be opened. This was nothing to do with a funeral taking place. He wanted to see what, if anything, had happened inside that tomb since he had personally sealed it the year before.

His seal was intact and had to be broken first before the slab could be moved. The Governor watched while this was done. Then he watched while the cement was removed, and the marble slab taken away from the entrance.

What was found was that Mrs Goddard's coffin was precisely where it had always been, but the other coffins were once more scattered around the tomb. Once again a coffin was standing on its end – that of Thomas Chase. *And there was not a mark of any sort on the sand*! It was if the coffins had moved by themselves through the air.

By now the Chase tomb had become notorious, and the family could stand it no longer. The family coffins were all taken out of the tomb and re-buried together in Christ Church graveyard in a special funeral ceremony. And there they still are.

The tomb itself was finally sealed up, with Mrs Goddard's coffin remaining alone inside it . . . and no one has entered it since.

The Haunted Submarine

Many sailors tend to be superstitious. Perhaps it is because of the sea's uncontrollable power, the sudden storms which can spring up, the uncertainty even in modern times. Or perhaps it is because some ships have been haunted. One in the Royal Navy was haunted by an officer who had been killed during the Second World War. Many of those on board saw him from time to time. He regularly appeared on the bridge – so regularly, in fact, that officers and crew, quite unafraid of his presence, would watch out for him.

There has even been a ghost ship, the *Flying Dutchman*. The last sighting of that appears to have been in 1942, when four people on the terrace of their home in Cape Town, South Africa, saw it sail across the bay and disappear from view as it passed behind Robben Island, in Table Bay.

The *Flying Dutchman* has been a legend since the seventeenth century, when its captain, Hendrick van der Decken, sailed from Amsterdam. While the ship was rounding the Cape of Good Hope, the southern tip of South Africa, a fierce storm sprang up. The legend is that Captain van der Decken made a pact with the devil to sail straight into the storm. His punishment was that he and his ship should sail on for ever without ever reaching land again.

There is an obvious flaw in this legend. How does anyone know that van der Decken made a pact with the Devil, since neither he nor any of his crew has ever spoken to a human since? Nevertheless, the phantom ship has apparently been seen several times over the centuries, and on one occasion in particular the evidence cannot be doubted.

A sixteen-year-old midshipman on board *HMS Inconstant* wrote in July, 1881: "At 4 am the *Flying Dutchman* crossed our bows." He went on to describe the sight: the strange ship was apparently glowing, and the masts, spars and sails, only about two hundred metres away from them, stood out absolutely clearly as it came up on their port (left-hand) side.

It might be assumed that at sixteen the midshipman was simply imagining things. But the *Flying Dutchman* was seen not only by him, but by the officer of the watch, the quarter-deck midshipman, and thirteen of the crew of *HMS Inconstant* and of two other ships which were sailing in the fleet.

The quarter-deck midshipman was sent forward to the forecastle to take a closer look, but by the time he arrived there the phantom ship had disappeared, having totally vanished in the clear night and calm sea.

So sixteen people saw this strange, old-fashioned ship sailing across in front of them that night in 1881.

And the one who wrote his report home about it might only have been sixteen, but he was also His Royal Highness Prince George, later to become George V of England. Another part of the legend is that disaster will overtake anyone who sees the phantom ship. Nothing happened to Prince George – but the seaman who had first sighted the *Flying Dutchman* fell to his death from the top of a mast later that same day!

But for a submarine to have the reputation of being haunted is a different matter entirely. Perhaps the only detailed account of one of those is the horrific story of the German submarine of the First World War, the UB65.

This was built in 1916, designed to accommodate three officers and a crew of thirty-one men. Even before it went into service with the German Navy, there was a series of disasters. During its construction a workman was killed by a falling girder. Three other workmen were killed by a fire in the engine room. On its sea trials a man was washed overboard and drowned. When it was submerged for its diving tests, an air tank sprang a leak and it remained submerged for twelve hours, during which time poisonous fumes began to spread through the vessel.

So far, this might have been purely an unfortunate coincidence that so many things had gone wrong, but already it was gathering a reputation as an unlucky vessel. This seemed to be confirmed on its return from its first expedition to sea. The submarine was loading torpedoes when one of them exploded, killing the second officer. He was buried at the military cemetery at Wilhelmshaven, and because of the damage the submarine had to go into dock for repairs.

After the repairs, and just before it was due to sail, one of the crew dashed into the officers' wardroom in a panic.

"The second officer has just come on board, sir!" he yelled.

"*This* is the second officer," said the Captain, indicating him. "What do you mean?"

"No – the second officer who was killed, sir!"

'That is quite impossible."

"But two of us saw him."

"So where is the other one who you claim saw this – ghost?"

"Hiding behind the conning tower, sir. We both saw him walk up the gangplank and come on board."

On deck, the other member of the crew who had been scared by the apparition was interviewed. There was no doubt – both of them had seen the dead second officer walk on to the submarine, then vanish.

As time went on, so many of the crew of the UB65 claimed to have seen the ghost of the dead man that the German High Command sent a Commodore to investigate. The Commodore questioned every officer and crew member. By the time his investigation had ended, almost every member of the crew had requested a transfer to another vessel – anywhere rather than remain on the UB65. And, strangely for wartime, all the requests were granted.

The Commodore's report led to the UB65 being taken out of service at Bruges in Belgium, for a minister of the Lutheran church to perform a service to exorcise the ghost. Then the entire ship's company, including those who had *not* asked for a transfer, was replaced.

For a ship, especially a ship in the German Navy, to be taken out of service so that an exorcism could take place, was unheard of before this time . . . an indication of how seriously the Commodore's report was taken. Something very strange indeed had certainly been going on for this step to be taken.

So now the submarine had a completely new crew and officers, and a captain who would stand no nonsense about ghosts and hauntings. He didn't believe a word of it, and not only that but even threatened punishment for any man on board who even mentioned a ghost. And for the time being, this seemed to work. UB65 went on two tours of duty totally without any visions of the dead man appearing on board, nor any other unfortunate incidents.

Then the captain was replaced, and as soon as this happened the ghost returned. Portland Bill is a point of land due south of Weymouth, in the English Channel. In January, 1918, UB65 was cruising fifteen miles from Portland Bill, in rough weather. The starboard lookout in the conning tower then noticed one of the ship's officers standing on the deck just below him, with the spray and waves crashing up around him.

Then the officer turned towards him. He wasn't one of the three who were supposed to be on board! The lookout yelled for the Captain, the Captain dashed across to see what was wrong, and also saw the figure, which then slowly vanished. The ghost had returned!

Four months later, in May, 1918, the submarine was operating first in the English Channel and then off the Spanish coast. During that month the ghost was seen three times. First a petty officer saw an officer whom he did not recognize enter the torpedo room and not come out again. When he went to investigate, there was no one there. The dead man

42

was seen twice more in the torpedo room by other people, and finally the torpedo gunner began to scream that the ghost would not leave him alone. The gunner jumped overboard and was drowned.

The end of this curious business came on 10th July, 1918. A submarine of the United States Navy was at periscope depth when it came across the UB65 on the surface. It prepared to attack, but before the torpedoes had even been launched the UB65 exploded – a "tremendous, almost unbelievable" explosion was how it was described. The German submarine sank, killing the entire crew.

There could be a logical explanation for its end. If the Captain of the UB65 saw the periscope of the American submarine, he would either decide to take avoiding action or he would have prepared to fire his own torpedoes. It did seem from its final position that the German Captain had ordered a counter-attack to take place. If there had been a fault in the torpedo tube causing a torpedo to explode the moment it was fired, that in turn might have made the rest of the torpedoes explode in a kind of chain reaction.

However, the torpedo room was where the ghost was seen most often. So there might be an almost unbelievable explanation of why the torpedoes exploded and finally sank the submarine.

The Watcher at the Gate

There is something odd about Makin-Meang. It is the most northerly of the Gilbert Islands, which lie in the Pacific Ocean, north-west of Australia. The Gilbert islanders regard Makin-Meang as a half-way house between the living and the dead.

Whenever a Gilbert islander dies, so the story goes, his ghost has to travel up the chain of islands until it reaches Makin-Meang. There it arrives on a beach at the south of the island, then has to walk right up to the northern end, which is known as the Place of Dread.

There sits Nakaa, the Watcher of the Gate, and in his hand he holds a terrible net. What he does with the net is strangle the ghosts, and so prevent them from passing through that Gate to Paradise. The only thing which can prevent Nakaa from doing this is for the family of the dead person to perform certain rituals over the dead body.

That was the story which Arthur Grimble was told

when he became a District Officer in the Gilbert Islands in 1916. Of course, he didn't believe a word of it. It was just a legend, even if it had been a legend for at least sixty generations of the islanders by the time he arrived there. It was just superstitious nonsense.

However, since his headquarters were actually on Makin-Meang, he began to ask questions. He found that the island had an eerie reputation right through the whole group of islands, for being a place full of ghosts. The local people, however, would tell him nothing at all when he asked. They would not even change the subject, but just remained silent – it was too dangerous even to talk about it to a stranger. His information came instead from an assistant, a man who came from the island of Tarawa. But even this man from Tarawa took great care never to risk the horror of meeting a ghost face to face.

"So how do you avoid meeting one?" Arthur Grimble asked.

"The Native Magistrate told me, when he saw I was scared," mumbled the assistant.

What happened was, he said, when the ghosts of people who had died on the other Gilbert islands arrived at Makin-Meang, they walked to the dreaded Nakaa along the road which ran above the beach on the western side of the island.

"But what about the people who die on Makin-Meang? Don't they go the same way?"

"No, they take the path on the eastern side instead."

So that meant there was a much greater risk of meeting ghosts on the west side than on the east, because more people died on the other islands than among the community living on Makin-Meang itself. If you went up to the Place of Dread, it didn't really matter which side of the island you walked, because you were going the same way as the ghosts. The only thing was that you must never, under any circumstances, look behind you!

Coming back, though, you must walk only along the eastern path – and you could find if that was going to be safe or not by asking first if any death was expected on the day you intended to use it.

By now Arthur Grimble was very curious, and wanted to see this Place of Dread for himself, so he asked the Native Magistrate to let him have a guide to show him the way to go.

At first the Magistrate flatly refused. "It's a very perilous place," he said.

"It won't be perilous for me, since I'm not a native," argued Arthur. "Anyway, I'm a Christian – the same as you. Surely you don't believe that souls have to go past Nakaa in order to get to Heaven?"

The answer was that these were not Christian ghosts but pagan ones, and they still walked the island. Even the Magistrate was scared, that was certain. Still, he did find for him a local police constable who was willing to show him the way – but only on strict conditions.

The first was that since Arthur Grimble was a stranger, he must go along the western path going towards the Place of Dread, the same as the ghosts of strangers did, and the second was that once they set off, no matter what, Grimble must not look behind him.

"What if I do look back?" asked Grimble.

"If you do, and you see a ghost, then you'll be dead within a year," replied the constable.

So they set off. It was quite a long journey, and after they had been walking for perhaps an hour, the constable took him into the trees at the side of the path and handed him a seed-coconut.

"What's this for?" asked Grimble, amused.

"You must carry it in both hands in front of you, because on your first visit to the Place of Dread you have to take a seed-coconut as a gift and plant it in Nakaa's grove," said the constable seriously.

So Grimble had to carry the enormous nut like that for another five miles, until they arrived at a place where the trees ended not far from the island's northern end. And there he had to plant it.

And that was when the constable refused to go any further with him. If Arthur Grimble really wanted to go any further, then he'd have to do it by himself.

When eventually Grimble arrived at the right place, he was rather disappointed. He had expected to find somewhere which was at least a little eerie. Instead it was just an area of bare rocks and sand. Because of the heat reflected from the sand and the rocks, by the time Grimble had walked back to where the constable was sitting waiting for him he felt rather disgruntled and very thirsty. It had hardly been worth the journey!

Since he hadn't been living on the island for long, he had not yet learned how to climb a forty-foot high tree to get himself a drinking nut, so he asked the constable to climb up and get one for him.

"I can't do that!" said the constable, horrified. "These trees belong to Nakaa!" Then he insisted that they should leave the place as soon as possible.

It had all been a waste of time, to Grimble's way of thinking. He might as well not have bothered to come. It hadn't been very interesting at all, this local bit of superstitious nonsense. And on top of that, he was now very thirsty indeed.

They started back along the eastern path. The constable would not walk with him now, but kept well behind.

"Are we out of Nakaa's grove yet?" Grimble called to him, hoping that before long the constable would at last be willing to find him something to drink.

"Not for another mile," the constable called back to him.

Before very long, Grimble saw another islander walking towards them. He was a man of about fifty, and he walked with a limp because his left foot was rather twisted. Round his middle he was wearing a decorated mat fastened by a belt, and he carried a scar on his left cheek. Grimble gave him a friendly greeting in passing.

The stranger, however, took no notice of him and just walked past. Arthur Grimble looked back, saw that the man was now just passing the constable, and called to him to ask the man to stop.

"What man?" asked the constable in surprise.

"Why, that one, the one who's just passed by you, of course."

The constable suddenly broke out into a sweat, which according to Arthur Grimble came out of his forehead and ran down into his eyebrows. Then he began to scream.

"I am afraid of this place!" he yelled. Then he put an arm across his face and ran off into the trees.

Grimble was left to find his own way back to the village. When he arrived there, hot, thirsty and cross, he found that the constable was already there before him. He was talking in some agitation to the Native Magistrate. Grimble went over to them at once to complain. This constable had pretended that he hadn't seen the man on the path, and was obviously trying to make him look a fool.

The Magistrate, however, remained unperturbed.

"Could you describe the man?" he asked calmly.

So Grimble did – including the twisted foot, the mat, the scar on his face . . .

"Then that would be Na Biria," said the Magistrate.

"Can't he speak, or something?" demanded Arthur Grimble.

"Well, not exactly. You see, he died this afternoon, at about three o'clock."

Grimble just didn't believe it – it could not have been the same man. But then he realized something. If the man had been dead for only an hour or two, the burial would not yet have taken place, so he would be able to see the body and then know for sure if he had really seen a ghost.

The constable objected at once. If a stranger appeared while the ceremonies were being performed, Na Biria would be certain to be strangled in Nakaa's net. That was how it was. The Magistrate, however, not being a pagan, said that he would take Grimble himself, if that was what he really wanted.

The body lay in the village. From a distance Grimble saw some of the villagers hitting the sides of the dead man's house with sticks, to frighten away any strange ghosts, while others sat with their arms raised at the head and feet of Na Biria's body.

As soon as Arthur Grimble had reached the edge of the circle of people beating at the house, he wouldn't go any further. It was the same man, all right. And if that was true, the rest of the legend might be true as well, and he didn't want to risk it.

I'll Come To You!

Lieutenant David McConnel, aged eighteen, was a trainee pilot at RAF Scampton, Lincolnshire. The date was 7th December, 1918.

"The Commanding Officer's just told me I'm to fly a Camel up to Tadcaster today," he announced to his friend, Lieutenant J.J.Larkin, who shared the same room. "I go later today. It's only sixty miles, so I'll see you at tea time. Don't scoff the lot before I get back!"

"I'll be seeing you, then," Larkin replied.

And David McConnel left the room as noisily as he always did, slamming the door and stomping off down the passage outside.

Later that same afternoon, Larkin was in the room reading. He heard McConnel's footsteps outside the door, then it opened noisily.

"Hello, boy!" McConnel called, as he always did.

Obviously he had returned from Tadcaster. Larkin glanced up from his book to see David in his flying clothes, as might have been expected, but what struck him as odd was that he was also wearing his Royal Navy cap. Naval lieutenant David McConnel had only recently transferred to the RAF.

They chatted for a short while, then McConnel said, "Well, cheerio!" and going out closed the door noisily behind him again.

It was too early for tea yet. Obviously David was going to report in. Not long afterwards, Lieutenant Garner-Smith came into the room. Larkin glanced at his watch, and it was a quarter to four.

"Has David come back yet?" asked Garner-Smith. "We've arranged to go into Lincoln tonight."

"Yes, he's back. He's just been in, a few minutes ago. I'm not sure where he's gone now, but I expect he'll soon be back again."

The shock came when Larkin was in the Albion Hotel, Lincoln, later that evening. He happened to overhear some other officers discussing the tragedy which had happened.

There had been dense fog over Tadcaster. David McConnel had somehow lost his way and had crashed in his Camel aircraft. A girl had heard the plane coming down and as soon as she had heard the crash had run towards it. She found a dead pilot inside, and had run for help. When the body was removed, it was found that his watch had stopped at 3.25 pm.

And yet, Larkin had been talking to him after he had opened the door and come into the room a few minutes after that time . . .

The Reverend Clarence Godfrey had been wondering for a long time about ghosts, and what they could possibly be. He wondered if it was possible for the ghost of a *living* person to appear. The only evidence would be if such a ghost could be made to appear to someone else. So on 15th November, 1886, he decided to try an experiment.

At a quarter to eleven that night he went up to his bedroom. It would be rather entertaining if he could make himself appear to a friend at the foot of her bed, to see what effect it had! So he concentrated hard on this with all the mental energy he could muster, trying to force his "spirit" to go into another person's bedroom. After about eight minutes he found that he suddenly felt extremely tired, so got into bed.

He awoke suddenly at 3.40 am the next morning, with a strange feeling that somehow he might have succeeded. He made a note of the time before he went back to sleep again. The next morning he asked his friend, who had not known of what he had been planning, if she had experienced anything unusual during the night.

"The strangest thing happened," she said. "I woke with a start at about half-past three this morning, for no good reason, and was sure that somebody else was in the room with me. I couldn't see anyone, so I lit a candle and looked about. There was nobody there, so I went downstairs to get myself a drink of soda water since I felt thirsty. And that's when it happened!"

"Go on," said the clergyman. "What happened?"

"You were there! I saw you, quite distinctly, standing on the stairs as I went back upstairs to bed."

The Reverend Godfrey was apparently standing on the staircase, in front of a large window, dressed as usual and looking as if he were concentrating on something, but with an unusually pale face. His apparition lasted for just three or four seconds before it disappeared. His friend had thought she had been dreaming it.

When the news of this remarkable experiment reached the Society for Psychical Research, they didn't believe it. But Clarence Godfrey was quite willing to repeat the experiment for their benefit. The first attempt was a complete failure, but they decided to try just one more time.

On 7th December, 1886, the Reverend Godfrey concentrated again, felt very tired, and went to bed. His friend reported the next day that she had heard a voice say, "Wake!" and felt a hand touching her head when she was waking up. Stooping over her was the Reverend Clarence Godfrey.

The interesting thing was that on both of the successful occasions Clarence Godfrey had no idea of how he had appeared, or what he had apparently been doing, until he was told about it afterwards.

In London in September, 1955, Lucien Landau felt ill and went to bed. In the same house lived a woman who later married Landau. Her room was opposite to his, on the other side of a landing.

The following morning Eileen told him that she had been worried about him, so in the middle of the night she had willed an apparition of herself to go into his bedroom to check how he was. His door had been shut, she said, but she had passed through it and found that he was, in fact, all right.

Naturally, Lucien Landau didn't believe a word of it.

"I won't believe that unless you can do it again," he said.

"And how would I be able to prove that I've done it?" asked Eileen.

Lucien looked around his room. His diary was lying on a table. "Take this into your room," he said, "then do it again tonight, only this time make your ghost bring this diary in with it!"

Eileen was doubtful. She didn't see how a ghost could be expected to be able to carry a solid object like a diary through two wooden doors.

"Then tonight, we'll leave both of our doors open," decided Lucien.

So that was what they did. It was not a very clever experiment, when you come to think of it. Eileen could simply have walked across the landing when she was sure that Lucien was asleep, taking the diary with her, have left it in his room and then returned to her own. Apparently Lucien hadn't thought of that possibility. But as it turned out, something very strange happened.

It was dawn the following morning, and Lucien Landau's room was just beginning to become lighter. Lucien woke up suddenly at a movement in his room to see Eileen, in her night-dress but with a very pale face, standing not far from his bed. While he watched the figure glided backwards towards the door.

Lucien promptly got out of bed and followed. The thought immediately struck him that it really could be Eileen, even if she was apparently gliding over the carpet instead of walking! But then he reached the point where he could see through the open door opposite that Eileen was lying in bed asleep, and the apparition – *both at the same time*. There was no doubt about it. The apparition vanished as soon as it reached the side of Eileen's bed.

When he returned to his room, he found instead of his diary a toy rubber dog on the table, which he knew belonged to Eileen.

He questioned her later that morning while they were having breakfast. She said that she had tried to pick up his diary from her room, but somehow hadn't been able to do that. So she had picked up her toy rubber dog instead. She could remember crossing the landing, to see Lucien fast asleep. She didn't remember anything at all about how she had got back to her own room, but she did remember putting the toy dog on to his table, thinking that would do instead of the diary!

The possibilities are very interesting, don't you think? But just suppose that *you* could send your ghost out of your body, what would happen if to your horror you found that you couldn't get back?

The Face in the Oven Door

It would be a terrible shock if one evening you happened to look into a mirror, to find a face in there which was not your own. But suppose you looked instead into the glass door of an oven, and found a face looking out at you from there. Not a head, just a face, trying to talk to you!

It really happened. Flight 401 from New York to Miami crashed in the Everglades of Florida in autumn, 1972, just before it was due to land. The aircraft was a Lockheed L 1011 Tri-Star carrying 176 passengers. 97 people died in the crash, together with the pilot, Bob Loft, and the flight engineer, Don Repo.

The reason for the crash appears to have started when an indicator light failed to come on to show that the nose-wheel had lowered and locked into position. So either the indicator bulb was faulty, or the nose-wheel had actually not lowered. To find out which was the cause, the pilot put the aircraft on to automatic pilot on a circling course while the flight engineer went to the observation bay to inspect the wheel position. In the meantime, the pilot checked the light bulb.

Bob Loft turned in his chair to remove the indicator light cover and unscrew the bulb, and in doing so it seems that by accident he knocked the switch for the automatic pilot and so turned it off. The aircraft plunged to the ground.

The plane, however, was not a complete write-off. The accident inspectors who investigated the crash found that some seats and the rear galley of the plane were capable of being salvaged, so these were sent to the Lockheed factory to be rebuilt, renovated, and then used again. These parts were then installed in a new Tri-Star which was under construction.

The galley at least was fitted into Tri-Star number 318. This aircraft flew early in 1973. On board, apart from airline staff being ferried home from other destinations, was a Vice-President of the Eastern Airlines company. Since an off-duty airline captain had been checked into the first-class compartment, the Vice-President went over to sit next to him and began to chat casually. Only when the supposedly off-duty captain turned and looked him full in the face did the Vice-President recognize him and realize . . . it was a dead captain of the L 1011, Bob Loft. There was no mistake!

The Vice-President left his seat in a hurry and went to summon the cabin staff. Even in his panic, what crossed his mind was that this might be an omen that some disaster was soon to take place! But when he returned with a stewardess, the seat where the apparition had sat was now empty.

The Vice-President, feeling rather foolish, thought

he could have been imagining what he thought he had seen. An off-duty captain really had been checked on board, but there was no evidence that he had been this particular one. And, of course, it was highly suspicious that only the Vice-President had seen the ghost – if that was what it was. The matter was glossed over as of no importance.

However, soon other inexplicable happenings began to take place on Tri-Star 318, which incorporated parts from the unfortunate Flight 401 disaster. A flight engineer entered the flight deck to make his instrument checks prior to a routine flight to Florida. He was surprised to find another uniformed flight engineer already there before him, sitting in his seat.

"You don't need to check the instruments. I've done that," the other said.

Then he turned towards him. It was unmistakably the dead flight engineer, Don Repo.

The flight engineer submitted a report on this affair. Some weeks later an Eastern Airlines captain checked the instruments himself before taking off from Miami to Atlanta, Georgia. Staring at him from the panel was the outline of Don Repo's face. He claims that he distinctly heard the words: "There will never be another crash on an L 1011. We will not let it happen."

Then on another occasion a pilot of the 318 saw both Bob Loft and Don Repo. At another time a stewardess, going to discover the cause of some smoke seen to be coming from a bulkhead during a flight, found herself facing the ghost of Bob Loft.

But so far, despite the report which was made each time, the ghosts had only been seen by one person at a time. Airline crew are not usually the sort to be given to imagining things which are not there. But there was always the possibility that by now perhaps they were *expecting* to see something strange, and consequently somehow doing so. And another point, of course, was that so far everyone who had seen a ghost on board the aircraft had known the living person previously.

But then something different happened.

The stewardess was Fay Merryweather, and the Tri-Star was carrying 180 passengers from New York to Florida. The seatbelt warning lights were switched off in the cabin, so now there were a couple of hours during which the in-flight meals could be served to the passengers. Stewardess Merryweather went into the galley.

When she reached for the handle of the oven door, looking out at her through the glass was a man's face, and the lips were moving as if they were trying to tell her something! She drew back in astonishment, and the face had gone. Naturally, she decided that she had imagined it, and reached for the door handle again. The face reappeared.

Not one to panic, she left the galley and walked briskly to the flight deck, to the seat of the flight engineer. "We have a problem," she said into his ear.

She would not explain what the "problem" was, but made her way back to the galley, with the flight engineer following her. At the door of the galley, before they went inside, she told him what she thought she had seen.

The face was still there. The flight engineer looked into the oven door and recognized the face of Don Repo, who by now had been dead for a year. What was more, when the face spoke now it could be heard. The exact words were reported as being: "Beware,

beware, fire in the jet."

Then both voice and face faded away.

But there was no fire in the jet, so what had happened did not seem to make sense. Neither of these two crew members flew in that same aircraft again, but a few months later it developed engine trouble on a flight to Mexico, so had to return to New York. After the repairs, as it took off on a test flight an engine burst into flames and only luck and the skill of the maintenance crew on board – according to the official report by the Federal Aviation Agency – managed to make sure that the plane landed without loss of life. Had the plane been carrying passengers, the report adds, there would have been a disaster.

Perhaps the ghost had the wrong occasion for there to be a fire in the jet, or perhaps it was an advance warning, or possibly there was no connection between the two events at all. But what is certain is that the Flight Safety Foundation studied the detailed reports of the ghost sightings, all given by "experienced and trustworthy pilots and aircrew", as the final report states, and all considered to be "significant".

The end came a year and a half after the first sighting had been reported. A technical officer with Eastern Airlines was given permission to hold a service of exorcism on board Tri-Star 318, because the company decided that something had to be done. The apparitions were appearing on board much more frequently now.

As the service took place, in the galley, aircrew said prayers while the officer sprinkled the galley with water. As he sprinkled it, the face of Don Repo appeared, staring at him, then faded slowly away. Neither he nor the ghost of Bob Loft was ever seen again.

The Everlastings

"Any errands you want me to do, Mrs Robinson?" asked Russell Hughes. He was fourteen and a Scout. He had been calling on Mrs Robinson since he was twelve, because Emma Robinson was a neighbour at Chicago Heights, Illinois, USA, and she was eighty years old.

"Why, thank you, Russell," said Mrs Robinson. She went to find her purse. It was an old, battered one.

"I'm making a purse out of leather, part of a Scout badge I'm working for," Russell remarked. "When it's finished, I'll give it you. You could do with a new one."

"Now that is generous," said Mrs Robinson, "but you don't have to trouble."

"It'll be no trouble," replied Russell.

Then shortly afterwards Mrs Robinson had a stroke and had to be taken into hospital. When she came out she was totally paralyzed down her left side and was confined to a wheelchair. She was a little disappointed that Russell had not been round to see her since her illness, but let it pass. She couldn't really expect a fourteen-year-old boy to spend a great deal of his time with an eighty-year-old widow, after all.

She was in the kitchen of her apartment in January, 1961, when she fell and found that she was unable to get up again. She struggled for a while, then began to shout for help. Not that there was much chance of anyone hearing her. She might be lying there for hours, because all the doors and windows were locked.

Then Russell appeared. He helped her up at once and put her into the wheelchair, then wheeled her out of the kitchen and into the living-room, where she could reach the telephone. Then he just went. Emma Robinson was surprised, because apart from not knowing how he had got into her apartment at just the right time, always before he would stay around and chat after he'd run an errand for her while Mrs Robinson fed him biscuits and milk. She just couldn't understand this at all.

She never saw Russell again. There was a good reason for this, as she found out soon afterwards – Russell Hughes, aged fourteen, had been killed in an accident with a motor scooter on 9th November, 1960 – two months previously!

But more was to come. Russell had finished making that leather purse before he had been killed. His parents had kept it in his bedroom, not knowing that he had promised it to Emma Robinson.

Two weeks after he had helped her into the wheelchair, Mrs Robinson woke one morning to find a leather purse, hand-made, lying at her side. Russell's parents had found that it had vanished, but had no idea of where it had gone, until they identified it.

This story is perfectly true – and so is another of where somebody appeared after he was dead. But this second account was so horrifying that for twenty-three years afterwards a group of men met annually to prevent it ever happening again.

Suppose that you hold a party one evening. Just a few friends are invited. The party takes place. Then suppose that a few days later you discover to your horror that one of the people who had attended your party had actually died several days before the party was held, but had apparently been there with you and your other friends all evening! That would be a nasty shock in itself, but actually it was worse than that . . .

At Jesus College, Cambridge, is a staircase rising from an angle in the building next to the hall of the College. It is called Cow Lane. At the top are some rooms which were used only as store rooms for nearly two hundred years, ever since the final meeting of the Everlasting Club. There was a very good reason for this.

In the eighteenth century, the Hellfire Club, founded by Sir Francis Dashwood, used to meet in a room in the church tower at West Wycombe, Buckinghamshire. It is said that they used to practise black magic there, and certainly one of their ceremonies was to drink out of a human skull. (That skull is now somewhere in the lake at Newstead Abbey, Nottinghamshire, where Lord Byron used to live.)

Not to be outdone, the Honourable Alan Dermot, son of an Irish peer, decided to set up a similar sort of club at Cambridge University, and he founded the Everlasting Club in 1738. There were only seven carefully chosen members. One was a young Cambridgeshire landowner, another a Cambridge doctor, and the rest were members of various Colleges at the University. All of them were between twenty-two and thirty years of age at the time.

There were certain peculiar rules for this Club, and the first was that the seven members, known as Everlastings, "may be either Corporeal or Incorporeal, as Destiny shall determine." That is, these seven would remain members of the Club for ever, even when they were dead! Alan Dermot was to be the "Everlasting President" of the Club, and its secretary.

A Minute Book was to be kept, and on 2nd November each year at ten o'clock at night they were all to meet for a special annual dinner, to be held each time in the home of that living member of the Club whose turn it happened to be. If anyone missed the dinner, then the President was to fine or punish him as he thought fit. And everyone present at each meal had to sign his name and write down his address in the Minute Book.

There was another rule which later became very important, for reasons which you will soon realize. If in any year at least four of the living members had any objection to the dinner taking place, then they had to meet and write an objection in the Minute Book not less than seven days beforehand. This was to be the only way it could be cancelled in any year.

So each year from 1738 the annual dinner was held. It was always a noisy affair, with shouting, swearing, a lot of drinking and, it is thought, with some sort of Devil-worship involved as well. And each year all seven of the members were present . . . until 2nd November, 1743, when the dinner was being held at the home of the Cambridge doctor.

Henry Davenport was missing that night. By now he was an officer in the British army and was at Dettingen, Germany, where a battle was about to take place. The Battle of Dettingen was on 3rd November, 1743, and Davenport was killed by a cannon ball.

Alan Dermot wrote in the Minute Book that Davenport was fined for failing to attend the dinner.

Then it became the morning of 3rd November, 1743, because these annual dinners went on for hours. In the book, Dermot wrote next: "Henry Davenport, by a cannon shot, became an Incorporeal Member, 3rd November, 1743."

He wrote this the day that Henry Davenport was killed. In those days there were no telephones, radios, news items on television, and no way of sending news to England except on horseback, then by sailing boat, then on horseback again or by coach. The news of the battle took days to reach England! Yet the Everlasting Club knew what had happened – that same day!

Could it have been that Davenport had actually *appeared* in his empty chair, slowly taking shape – something like the way Sir George Tryon had appeared in Eaton Place, London, at the same time as he died in the Mediterranean in 1893?

We can't be sure, since none of the members would speak about it afterwards. Because something far worse happened at the same time, and when the members discovered what it was, they were absolutely terrified.

All the members present had to sign their names and write their addresses, because that was another of the rules. At the top of the list for that fateful dinner the President wrote: "Alan Dermot, President," and gave his address as "at the Court of His Royal

Highness". Dermot was actually a supporter of Bonny Prince Charlie – Prince Charles Edward Stuart, the Young Pretender, who claimed to be the rightful King of England. Prince Charles Edward Stuart was in Paris at the time, and Dermot was there with him in October, 1743. He was killed in a duel in Paris on 28th October, 1743 – *five days before the Club met!*

Yet at the dinner, after he was dead, he was present, fined Henry Davenport, and wrote his name and present address in the Minute Book! Beyond all doubt, it was the unmistakable handwriting of Alan Dermot in the Minute Book.

In fact, on 10th November there was written by the next Secretary of the Club: "This day was reported that the President was become an Incorporeal in the hands of a French chevalier. The Good God shield us from ill." And that last entry shows how scared the surviving members had now become, considering the sort of activities in which they were usually involved!

The news that they had dined with a dead man, and hadn't realized it, shattered the Everlasting Club. So now they took great care to meet every year in October, well before the seven-day deadline in the rules, and solemnly objected to holding the dinner that year. And this went on for five years.

Then another member died. Only four of them were left now, and if there were fewer than four, then they would have to hold the dinner again, for all seven members whether they were alive or dead.

Regularly for eighteen more years the survivors met to record that they objected to holding the dinner, dreading what was likely to happen if it ever took place again. By now they were all middle-aged men, and knew that sooner or later the inevitable was bound to happen – one of them was bound to become the next "Incorporeal", or dead member of the Club.

Then on 27th January, 1766, the Secretary at the time, Francis Witherington, died. The Minute Book was delivered to James Harvey, the next in line to be the Secretary, the same day. Harvey died within a month. The book was then delivered to the next in line, William Catherston. He was dead two months later, on 18th May. The last survivor of the Everlasting Club was now Charles Bellasis, because he was the only "Corporeal Member" left.

The situation by now might have seemed desperate, but Bellasis had no intention of dying, and what was more, he intended to defy the Club rules. Charles Bellasis by now was a respectable Fellow of Jesus Club, where he gave lectures to the students. He lived in the rooms at Cow Lane where the Everlasting Club had first met.

On the night of 2nd November that year he stayed in his rooms at Cow Lane, closed the door and barricaded himself in.

At exactly ten o'clock that night there was suddenly an uproar from Cow Lane. There were shouts, yells, songs suddenly bursting out, blasphemies, the crashing of glass, the sound of furniture breaking – and all of it was heard by the professors and lecturers in Jesus College, by the students, by the Master of the College in his house, and by the College servants. Yet no one dared to climb the stairs of Cow Lane to the rooms at the top. The uproar stopped at midnight.

Still nobody dared go to find out what had been going on. But at dawn the next day they decided to find out. When there was no answer from inside the rooms, a sledgehammer was sent for and the door broken down.

Bellasis was dead in a chair at the end of the long oak table, with his arms across his face as if he had been trying to avoid seeing something. Round the table were six other chairs, as though set out for a dinner. Some of them were upside down, others were smashed. Broken glass and crockery lay on the table and scattered around the floor.

On the table in front of Charles Bellasis was the leather-bound Minute Book, with next to it a quill pen, a silver ink pot, and the sand sprinkler which in those days was used instead of blotting paper to dry ink. In the book, for the first time since 1742, were written the names of all *seven* members of the Everlasting Club, but with no addresses alongside them.

The President, Alan Dermot, had written in the book, in his own unmistakable handwriting, in Latin, that Bellasis was "fined" for failing to provide a meal as the rules required.

That was the final end of the Everlasting Club. No on dared to live in those rooms until at least 1940, near the beginning of the Second World War, and until then they were used only for storage. The rooms are still there, and are now in use again.

They should be quite safe – after all, those who now live there since Charles Bellasis died cannot possibly become members!

The Sign of the Bird and the Beast

If the Devil walked the earth, according to legend he might have horns and cloven hooves. Perhaps. It seems a little unlikely. And yet . . . there have been mysterious footprints which have appeared, belonging to invisible and impossible creatures, and there's been no doubt whatever of their existence. Let's start with the bird.

Two men sat alone in a room in Lincoln's Inn, London, not speaking, waiting for something to happen. Two other rooms led off this one, with the only way in or out of them through the closed doors which now faced them. There was no furniture, for that had been removed, and the bare floors of all three rooms were now covered in powdered chalk. There were no cupboards, and they had checked most carefully for hidden or secret panels. The walls had been white-washed. In each of the three rooms bare light bulbs were burning brightly. It was a moonlit night in May, 1901.

The two men were Ralph Blumenfeld, News Editor of the *Daily Mail*, and another reporter, Max Pemberton (later to become Sir Max Pemberton, Chairman of the *Daily Express* newspaper group), and they were hoping for a news story. What they had taken with them into the room where they now sat was a card table and two chairs. With them they had brought some sandwiches, something to drink, writing material, their pipes, tobacco and matches, and both of them wore a watch.

They were there because for years a "ghostly presence" was said to appear at midnight in that room, and at least eight tenants had left in a hurry in the previous two years alone! The last tenant of the rooms had been a friend of Blumenfeld's, and he had departed as quickly as all the others. The two men had rented the rooms for just twenty-four hours, and now they sat as midnight approached and waited, not knowing at all what to expect.

Midnight came and went. Nothing happened at all. Then they heard one of the door latches click.

"12.43 am," Blumenfeld jotted down in his notebook, "the latch clicked, the brass handle turned, and slowly the door swung open to its full width." That was how the account appeared in the *Daily Mail* on 16th May, 1901.

At 12.56 am, the other door clicked and opened in the same way. They waited, but when nothing else seemed about to happen both of them got up from the card table and went over and closed the two doors again, but not before standing in each doorway and looking carefully round the other two rooms. Both of these were still brightly lit, there were no marks on the floors in either of them, no other way in, and no draughts could be felt.

Just over half an hour later, at 1.32 am, the right-hand door opened a second time, taking eleven seconds (they timed it!) to swing right open. Five minutes later, at 1.37 am, the left-hand door opened. From where they sat, they could now see right into the two rooms.

At precisely 1.40 am, both doors started to close again together, then just before they were nearly closed they suddenly slammed shut. And between 1.45 am and 1.55 am the same thing happened again.

Then there was a short period during which there was complete silence. But in the two minutes beginning at 2.07 am, the final opening of the doors occurred, only this time instead of closing they remained wide open, almost as if something invisible was having a game with them.

But now they could see in the white chalk covering the floor in the left-hand room three large footprints had appeared, as if made by some huge bird, and in the right-hand room five of the same footprints. They led across the rooms diagonally towards the doors leading to the centre room in which they were sitting. Each print had three toes, with a short spur behind – "like a turkey's footprint", they reported.

They stayed still for at least twenty minutes, waiting for whatever was going to happen next. But nothing did, and both of the doors remained wide open. They decided that the show was over. So they got up, measured the footprints (7 centimetres long), drew sketches of them, lit their pipes, packed up and went home.

Soon afterwards the building was demolished and another built to take its place. Nothing like this ever happened in the new building, nor were any more "ghostly presences" reported.

There is no explanation. The facts are exactly as the two newspaper men reported them. Doors opened and closed by themselves, the footprints of the unknown bird appeared from nowhere, and that it is. But what sort of bird made those marks has never been identified, even if they did seem to belong to something like a turkey, and it all happened not mysteriously and strangely in dark surroundings but in a room painted white and with all the lights on.

But this was not the only time that strange footprints have appeared. The difference is that on the other occasions they were definitely made by some sort of animal. But since their first appearance those other marks have been known as "the Devil's footprints".

On the night of 8th February, 1855, snow covered most of the county of Devon. When people woke that morning they were surprised to find footprints in the snow, looking something like the marks left by a donkey. They were about ten centimetres long by about six centimetres wide), with twenty centimetres between them, sometimes just a little more.

But the footprints were in a *single* line, as if made by a *two-legged* donkey marching forward with one hoof always exactly in front of the other. Something like a donkey, but with only two legs? Or a creature with only one foot, hopping? And running in an unbroken line for fifteen miles from Totnes to Exmouth?

The footprints stretched in a straight line across farms, over gardens, along lanes, and where there was an obstacle in the way, such as a building or a hayrick, over the roofs. Where there was a wall in the way, and one such wall was three metres high, the marks stopped at one side and immediately re-appeared on the other, as if the wall had not been there at all. When a river was crossed, the marks led to the bank of the river, and then carried on on the far side.

Because there was a severe winter in 1855, the marks remained in the snow for days, and hundreds of people saw them. Various explanations were made at the time, once the people had got over their initial fear, varying from an unknown animal which had escaped from a zoo, to an unknown monster which had come ashore from the sea, to the Devil himself.

The depth of snow that night was about nineteen millimetres, leaving on its surface the marks of such other animals as dogs, cats, rabbits and birds. The marks appeared also on a window-sill at Marley House near Exmouth which was two storeys up the building and in the middle of a field near Exmouth there was an inexplicable break in the line – the marks appeared in the middle of the field, all pointing in the same direction "without any apparent approach or retreat" according to the Reverend Ellecombe of Clyst St George, who also found them.

Another point was that each footmark removed the snow from underneath it as if the ground had been branded by a hot iron. And also in one place it was found that the tracks spread wider and doubled, then turned back into a single track as before, with four white, oblong droppings the size and shape of a large grape in the centre. The marks finally melted away with the snow after three days.

But this was not the only time that the marks have been seen. The last recorded time was again in Devon, in February, 1963. They did not stretch so far on this occasion, but were seen, measured and sketched by two people who lived at Mannamead, and by another in Noss Mayo. The woman in Noss

Mayo actually heard "a terrifying howl" from just outside her house at about eight o'clock that night, while she was having a bath. Living in the countryside, she knew the sounds made by all the animals such as foxes, but could not identify this sound at all – except, she said, that it was so horrible that she never wanted to hear anything like it again!

There is no logical explanation for either the bird or animal footmarks, and the more the logical possibilities are looked into, the more impossible any explanation becomes.

There is, of course, one interesting point: these marks appeared because there was powdered chalk on the floor of those rooms in Lincoln's Inn, and because there was snow on the ground in Devon. Supposing there was no chalk, or no snow. The marks would not then appear. But the *thing* would still be there, simply not leaving marks behind it. In fact, is it possible that some sort of creatures walk about regularly at night, and we don't know about it?

The Phantom Battle

Edge Hill is a place which lies almost exactly on the border of the two counties of Warwickshire and Northamptonshire. Here in the year 1642 one of the battles of the English Civil War between King Charles I and the Parliamentary army took place. Years before, King John had fought a battle there with his barons, too, before he signed the Magna Carta.

What happened after the Battle of Edge Hill was so amazing and unbelievable that Charles I ordered an enquiry just a few months later. The officers who investigated didn't believe what they had been told, either – until they found themselves seeing it and hearing it for themselves. And what's more, although it has faded with time, it is still sometimes seen and heard today!

The battle took place on Sunday, 23rd October, 1642. Although afterwards both sides claimed a victory, the truth was that the King's army had lost.

This was largely because of Prince Rupert of the Rhine, King Charles's nephew. He was a brilliant cavalry leader, but unfortunately for the King once he had led a cavalry charge he never knew what to do next, and had no idea of swinging the horses round and rejoining the battle. He was, in fact, rather hot-headed and impetuous.

On this occasion, he led a cavalry charge, which as usual was completely successful, then his troops on horseback found that they had charged right through to the supplies of the Parliamentary army and they spent time plundering it instead of going back to rejoin the fighting. By the time they did return, the King's troops were withdrawing from the battlefield, and the King himself retreated to Oxford.

Two months later it was Christmas week. On Christmas Eve some shepherds, farm labourers and a few late travellers were around just after midnight when they were scared by the sound of a battle going on near them.

Then they saw the battle – infantry, cavalry, the jangle of harness, charging and neighing horses, powder smoke from the guns, they heard the musket fire, the cannon fire, the cries of men, even the trumpets giving orders. They even saw the flames coming from the muskets and cannons as they were fired. The noise was so loud that birds were woken up and flew off, and cattle stampeded. And it lasted not just for a short time, but for several hours, until about three o'clock the next morning.

On that Christmas night, many people from the surrounding villages went out to watch, in hopes of seeing the battle again – and were not disappointed! It was all happening again. And it repeated itself the following Saturday and Sunday nights as well, and again the weekend after that.

When the astonishing news reached Charles I in Oxford, he ordered an immediate enquiry. He sent a commission of officers back to Edge Hill to investigate these totally unbelievable reports. Their findings were printed at the King's command on 23rd January, 1643. The ones whom he sent were Colonel Lewis Kirk, Captain Dudley, Captain Wainman, and three members of his Court.

The members of the commission expected to find the whole affair a fake, until they started taking evidence from some of the local people. They were a little less sceptical still when they heard the same story from the local Church minister, the Reverend Samuel Marshall, and the local magistrate, William Wood. Both of these said that they had seen the phantom battle for themselves.

But what finally convinced them was when the battle started again, with them present. They recognized some of the apparitions, even, including Sir Edmund Verney, the King's standard bearer, who had been killed in the fighting. His hand had been cut off, still holding the standard. They found that they could even watch the entire progress of the battle, which while they had been taking part themselves they had not, of course, been able to see so clearly.

At the beginning, they reported, the King's army seemed "to have the best", but after two hours "the King's colours withdrew, or rather appeared to fly" – that is, the Parliamentary army drove the King's army from the battlefield. "What this doth portend God only knoweth," the report continues.

As if this was not astonishing enough, having happened beyond all doubt since so many people had both seen and heard it, including all the disbelieving members of the commission which Charles had sent to investigate – it has been seen since. When it happens, it is always on the anniversary of the battle now, but there is no doubt that it has faded with time, as if the effect is wearing away.

One woman in recent times was so astonished at what happened to her near the battlefield that she gave a detailed account on BBC radio of her strange experience. She had been driving in her car along a road on the way to visit some friends, when she suddenly heard strange sounds going on all around her – happy sounds, cheerful voices and some shouting. It sounded, she said, almost as if some kind of party was going on invisibly outside her car.

Then to her astonishment and fright a man's laughing head appeared without warning part-way between the car windscreen and the end of the car bonnet! Then it faded. Going back home the next day, at the same spot she could hear this time groans and cries around her, as if people were in agony, but this time she saw nothing, just heard the noises.

Only afterwards did she find that she had been driving without realizing it along the road which runs near the edge of the battlefield, on the eve and then the day of the anniversary of the Battle of Edge Hill.

What she had encountered were the ghosts of the troops, all happy and cheerful, on the anniversary of the day before the battle had taken place, then coming back the following day the end of the battle was being repeated, with the wounded and dying all around, and the bloodshed over.

This is the only authentic ghostly battle to take place, as far as is known, anywhere in the world, and there is no doubt that the battle has repeated itself in ghostly form several times since and that it is absolutely genuine.

But it wasn't the only ghostly appearance in the English Civil War. Charles I himself saw a ghost, only at first he thought it was just a nightmare which he was having. But the second time, he was quite convinced.

On 12th May, 1641, Charles had signed the death warrant of Thomas Wentworth, Earl of Strafford. He had no real choice in the matter. The war had not yet begun, the mob were outside St James's Palace, Whitehall, in London, and if he hadn't signed the warrant his own life, the lives of his family and the stability of his kingdom would have been at great risk. So reluctantly he signed the warrant for the Earl of Strafford's death, and a hundred thousand people watched Stafford's execution in glee.

The fact was that the Earl of Strafford did not deserve to be put to death. At one time his job had been Lord President of the North, and in the north of England he had stamped out slave labour in the woollen mills, championed the apprentices, and had come down very heavily on any arrogant landowners or greedy lawyers. After that, when he became Lord Deputy of Ireland, he did the same thing. He was sometimes harsh with his equals, but invariably was considerate with humbler people. He hated double-dealers and those who used the King's Court simply to make fortunes for themselves.

What he wanted was a sensible monarchy working with a Parliament which was free to represent the people. In fact, at one time he had gone to prison. He had refused to pay a special tax which the King had imposed in 1626, because he considered that the

King had no right to impose a tax without Parliament's approval first. So what with one thing and another, he made many enemies both at Court and in Parliament – and that was what really led to his death.

However, four years later, Charles I was staying at a house in Daventry, Northamptonshire – it's still there, and is now the Wheatsheaf Inn. Two hours after the King had gone to bed, his guards heard an argument going on in the bedroom, and distinctly heard two separate voices, one the King's and one belonging to somebody else.

They burst into the room, in case the King was being attacked, but Charles said that he had dreamed that Strafford had been there, and had told him not to fight the Parliamentary army any more, for he would never defeat them.

The next morning the King called a council and told the members what he had dreamed. Then he announced there would be no more war, and instead they would move north. Prince Rupert was a member of the council, and said that they should not be put off just because the King had had a bad dream.

That same night, Strafford appeared again, in armour, with a thin line of blood across his neck where the executioner's axe had cut through it. He warned Charles again not to fight, said that the King's army would be defeated if he did, and that it would all end in Charles's own execution. It was, the ghost said, the last advice that he was permitted to give him.

So the morning after, Charles called another council, and reported what had happened at this second appearance. He was now convinced it was no dream. "My Lord Strafford was there!" he announced, as the record of the council meeting shows.

Again, Prince Rupert was scornful. Unlike the other officers, of course, the Prince was a member of the King's family and could speak exactly as he wished.

So on 14th June, 1645, the Battle of Naseby took place. The King's army was defeated, and the Civil War was virtually at an end.

"I wish to God I had paid heed to the warning," Charles often said afterwards, while he was waiting for his own execution. Those who had been with him during those two nights in Daventry at least knew exactly what he meant.

The Oldest Ghost

The man on horseback appeared out of the pine wood and galloped towards the road. Then he turned his horse and began to gallop parallel with the road instead. It was a country area so people on horseback are not exactly unusual, even today. The place was Bottlebush Down in Dorset.

What was unusual was the way the man was dressed, and how he was riding. His legs were bare, he wore a long, loose cloak, and in his hand he was carrying or waving some sort of weapon. His horse had no bridle or stirrups.

Then he just vanished! Neither horse nor rider was there any more.

A pre-historic barrow is a mound of earth which at one time was used as a burial chamber, and this particular part of England is littered with them, because the area was a thriving community in the days before the Saxons invaded Britain. Where the horse and rider disappeared was near one of those ancient barrows.

The man who watched, fascinated, was Mr R.C.C. Clay, who lived near Salisbury. At the time he was in charge of excavations being made by the Society of Antiquaries at a Late Bronze Age burial ground near Bournemouth. The Bronze Age lasted in Britain from about 2,000 BC to about 600 BC, and what fascinated Mr Clay especially was that, from his expert knowledge, he knew that the horseman was dressed as if he belonged to the Late Stone Age period, somewhere between 800 BC and 600 BC.

Clay was in his car at the time. He used to drive to the excavation site at Pokesdown each afternoon from Salisbury, then drive back home again at dusk, and he saw the horseman as he was driving home one evening. Because the horseman had been riding towards the road, he had slowed down to let him cross, but then when the horseman had turned he had kept pace with him along the road so that he had plenty of time to observe him closely. After all, he was only about fifty metres away from him at the time.

So Clay began to make a few enquiries among the people who lived in the area, to find if anyone else had ever seen this strange sight. It turned out that the horseman was well known. As one old shepherd asked him, "Do you mean the man on horseback who comes out of the opening in the pine wood?" The shepherd knew the ghost well, and after the first shock had grown used to seeing him riding across the downs, often very close to him and always along the same route. He was quite harmless, he said. The horseman had been seen so often, in fact, that several other local people had grown quite used to his appearance, and thought nothing of it.

A few years later, there was actually a complaint to the police about him! Two girls had been cycling to a dance in the area when they suddenly found a strange man on horseback following them over the downs.

The horseman's existence was not known outside of the county of Dorset, however, until August, 1956, when James Wentworth Day wrote a letter to the *Salisbury Journal* to ask if anyone had ever heard of any true stories of any pre-historic ghost, since as far as he knew there was no such thing. Mr Clay wrote to him to say that in fact there certainly was one.

The horseman's ghostly ride is a legend now, and is the only authentic, pre-Saxon, Ancient British ghost known to be in existence.

The Ghost Who Didn't Believe in Ghosts

Oscar Wilde once wrote a story called *The Canterville Ghost*. In it, in order to keep up appearances, the rather unsuccessful ghost had to resort to such things as using red paint to touch up the ghostly blood-stains, because they kept wearing out. The truth, however, can be even stranger than that.

When Matthew Manning first met Robert Webbe, Matthew was sixteen, but Robert was more than three hundred years old. They both lived in the same house at Linton, Cambridgeshire. The difference was that Robert Webbe was born in the house in 1678, while Matthew and his family were living in the house in 1971. It is perhaps the most bizarre true ghost story ever.

"A burglar!" thought Matthew when he saw the figure going up the staircase.

Then he realized that it couldn't possibly be a burglar. For one thing, the man was wearing a green frock coat with large pockets, frilled ruffs and a cream cravat. For another he wore a wig such as men did in the early eighteenth century. Also he was walking up the stairs with the aid of a couple of walking-sticks.

Matthew began by being scared when he realized what he was really seeing, but this turned to astonishment at once. For the ghost turned and looked at him. And then spoke!

"I must offer you my most humble apology for giving you so much a fright," the ghost said, "but I must walk for my blessed legs."

Matthew grabbed a used envelope and a pencil and on the back of the envelope drew a sketch of him. The ghost seemed to be waiting while he did that, then it turned, walked slowly up the stairs and disappeared.

On other occasions when the ghost appeared, he was usually complaining about his "troublesome legs". Matthew's father, Derek Manning, who was an architect, also became involved with the ghost. He was often woken with a feeling that somebody had climbed into his bed and was somehow superimposing another body on his own. Very often he could even hear the scratching of a man's not very well shaven face on the sheets next to him. And every time he felt a prickling, tingling sensation in his lower right leg which would then spread to affect his left leg as well, rather as if he were starting to suffer from gout, which is a painful disease of the feet and legs. This, it was decided, was probably what Robert Webbe had suffered from.

Then Matthew suddenly discovered that he was able to write automatically, a thing he had never been able to do before. All he had to do was hold a pen or pencil in his hand, have some blank paper in front of him, concentrate, and some sort of power would take over and write messages on the paper as if his hand were being controlled by somebody else's mind. This turned out to be rather useful – and entertaining.

Robert Webbe, he discovered, had had the front part of the house added to the original building in 1730. Then he himself had died there in 1733. The front part of the house was where he was usually to be seen, but he was likely to appear anywhere in the building.

In July, 1971, in a period of six days more than five hundred names and dates got themselves mysteriously written on the walls of Matthew's bedroom, in various types of handwriting, and always in pencil. Most of the names and dates came from Robert Webbe's own lifetime, but others covered a period stretching as far back as 1355 and as late as 1959.

It could be suspected that Matthew wrote these himself, possibly without even knowing it. What is certain is that nobody was ever seen doing it, and it was only after some of the names and dates were checked by some research into the local history of the area that they were found to be accurate. So Robert Webbe had to be behind the writing somehow.

Then other things began to happen, as well. The family would suddenly find there was a strong smell of pipe tobacco out of nowhere, which was odd since nobody in the house smoked. Footsteps could be heard coming from empty rooms. Quite often the family would be surprised to hear a hand bell ringing in the hallway when there wasn't a hand bell anywhere in the house. Sometimes they could smell old and musty books, and even once or twice the stench of rotting fish!

Things disappeared. Some old prints hanging on the wall of the house vanished, a scarf, and a fifty pence piece from a money box. It seems that Robert

Webbe was not too sure about the fifty pence piece, because later that reappeared lying on the stairs. In exchange, strange, old-fashioned or antique objects began to *appear*, again on the stairs, as if they had been put there deliberately so that they could be found easily.

Other curious things which happened was that Matthew's parents' bed was found with the covers pulled back, and the pillow dented as if somebody had been laying his head on it, perhaps having a little rest! On one occasion a pair of pyjamas were left neatly folded beneath a pillow, with the buttons left unfastened, and when they were taken out they had been neatly buttoned up.

Matthew, through his new-found power of automatic writing, demanded to know what was going on, and Robert Webbe said that he was causing it. What was more, it was his house, he said, and he could do what he liked in it.

When Matthew one day came across him face-to-face in his parents' bedroom, he tried to shake hands with him. It was eerie, he reported, when he found that his outstretched hand passed clean through the hand of the ghost. Matthew then decided to give the ghost a present. He went out to collect a doll's wooden clog which belonged to his sister, went back and held it out to the ghost in his hand. The ghost took it from him and slipped it into a pocket of his coat.

That was peculiar enough, but what happened next surprised even Matthew, who by now, with the entire family, was getting used to peculiar things happening. The ghost of Robert Webbe slowly faded away, and the toy clog vanished with him and never appeared in the house again.

From "conversation" with the friendly ghost, Matthew learned that Webbe had been a trader in grain who had been very proud of his house and the way in which he had enlarged it. But he died only three years after it was completed, and he'd rather wanted to take his house with him when he died!

Matthew's conclusion was that this must be the reason why he reappeared at all. "I think that it is why he is going round and round in a strange sort of time loop . . . From time to time, someone in the house provides him with enough psychic energy to allow him to make contact."

Possibly the oddest thing in the whole curious affair happened when Matthew once made contact with him to ask some questions about the history of the local area. The question of local ghosts came up. Robert Webbe said that he didn't believe in ghosts, and not only that, but for certain there were none in his house!

There is another house where perhaps the apparitions don't realize they are ghosts. This house has two friendly ghosts; they are two little four-year-old girls, who died fifty-eight years apart, although they still seem to play together.

Another thing which is very strange is that when Mr and Mrs Rugless, who retired to live in the house in Farway, Devon, find the noise of them playing is getting too much, Mrs Edna Rugless just shouts up the stairs, "Children, please play more quietly!" – and they do.

It's a 300-year-old farmhouse, and the children run around upstairs. Every now and then there's a creaking noise as if they're playing on a wooden rocking-horse. One afternoon they grew rather naughty and started jumping about on the landing, so Mrs Rugless went out into the hall and shouted up the stairs to them to stop it. And they did.

No one knows why the ghosts appeared, but as soon as Mr and Mrs Rugless moved in the noises began in one of the bedrooms almost immediately, and their pet dog and cat refused to go anywhere near it.

Then a friend stayed with them on holiday. The friend was interested in psychic happenings, so without telling her anything of what they had experienced, Mrs Rugless asked her if she could feel anything special in their house. The friend told her that somewhere in the house were the spirits of two little girls, aged four or five, and one of their names began with an E and the other with an A.

Mrs Rugless went to see the local vicar, the Reverend Frederick Gilbert, and they checked the parish register, which records all christenings, marriages and deaths in the parish. Two little girls had actually died in the house where Mr and Mrs Rugless now lived, a girl called Elizabeth in 1844, and a girl named Anne in 1902. There was no doubt now about who the girls were.

Mr Bill Rugless was not happy to find that they had moved into a haunted house at first, but when he discovered that the ghosts were neither frightening nor eerie, in fact just a couple of "pleasant little spirits", as he called them, he changed his mind. Not only that, he thinks that they're lucky to have them living with them!

The Chimney Sweep

"Grandpa Bull!" shouted the youngest member of the family, a girl aged five.

By now no one was surprised, because they had all seen him around the house. The trouble was that he had been dead for eight months.

Samuel Bull was a chimney sweep who lived with his wife, Jane, and their twenty-one-year-old grandson, James, in a rented cottage in Oxford Street, Ramsbury in Wiltshire. He died of cancer in a bedroom of the cottage on 21st June, 1931.

Two months later one of their daughters, Mrs Edwards, together with her husband and their five children, moved in with Mrs Jane Bull. It was not a good move. The house was too small for all of them, but it was the early 1930's when money was short. Before long, to make the situation worse, the house, which had never been in a very good condition, began to deteriorate. Some of the rooms actually became unfit for habitation, and the whole family were soon living in squalor.

The Vicar of Ramsbury became involved in trying to have the family moved into a council house instead. Once they had moved out the owner of the cottage intended to have it put back into good condition, but until alternative housing became available there was nothing he could do.

In February, 1932, some of the children complained to their mother that they kept hearing someone outside their bedroom door at night, and it was scaring them. Three of them had been sleeping in their grandmother's room, but when two of them caught influenza they were moved into a downstairs room instead where they could be kept warmer.

Then the third of the children, Mary Edwards, aged thirteen, also caught influenza, and while her mother was with her they both saw Grandpa Bull appear. A little later the dead man was seen to go up the stairs and pass through a closed door into the room in which he had died. This had been the room in which Mrs Bull had been sleeping, until it became unfit to live in and so was shut up.

Then Mrs Edwards and the grandson, James, saw the ghost together, and this time Mrs Bull was told about the apparition. Mrs Bull, however, was not surprised at the news. She had seen him several times already, when she was lying in bed. Every time he had gone over to her and laid a hand on her forehead, even once speaking to her and calling her name. What Mrs Bull noticed particularly was the state of her late husband's "poor hands", because the knuckles almost seemed to be sticking out through the skin.

Before long the whole family had seen the ghost of Samuel Bull, not just once but several times, and of course the village came to hear of it. One of those who did was Admiral Hyde Parker. He mentioned it to Lord Selborne, in April of that year, who in turn mentioned it to Lord Balfour. And before long, Lord Balfour and a Mr J.C. Piddington, who were both interested in the mystery, arrived in Ramsbury to find out what was really happening.

They called on the Vicar, who had already made some enquiries himself. He asked the members of the family whether any of them believed in spiritualism or anything of that sort. They didn't believe in it. What was more, this was the first time that any of them had experienced anything like this. It had come as a complete surprise – and shock!

By the time Lord Balfour and Mr Piddington had arrived at Ramsbury, on 14th April, 1932, the family were getting ready to move out. A council house had been found for them. The only furniture left in the cottage by then was in the room where Mrs Bull, who was ill, was lying. She was going to be the last one to be moved into their new home.

Mrs Bull told the two men that when the ghost had first appeared, it had frightened her much more than it seemed to have done the children. It was so completely life-like, she said. She had expected a ghost to glide, because that was what she had heard that they did. But Samuel Bull walked, and seemed perfectly solid, like a real person. That was what had frightened her so much the first time. And always it looked exactly as her husband had done when he had returned home from chimney-sweeping each evening.

What was more, the figure didn't just appear to her and then vanish, nor did it do that with any others in the family. As Mrs Edwards pointed out, her dead father was more often than not there in the house with them for at least half an hour at a time, just moving among them but not taking notice of any of them apart from Mrs Bull. In fact, the family became so used to the presence that before long they were not in the least alarmed. One of them actually said that he was "a bit of a bore"! They also said they could always tell when something was going to happen, perhaps half an hour before it did. They all had a strange sort of feeling first.

The cottage in which the Bulls lived is no longer there. The last appearance of the ghost was on 9th April, five days before the family moved out. The cottage itself was destroyed during the Second World War and a shop with a flat above it stands where it once was.

Most of the other house hauntings which have taken place this century – and there have been plenty of them! – have started for no obvious reason, not involving members of the families of the people living there.

Number 11, West Grove, Askern, in Yorkshire suddenly became haunted early in 1957, when Mr and Mrs Holt moved into it. Mrs Holt woke one night to see a figure bending over their child's cot. When she roused her husband, the figure disappeared into the fireplace! Although the Holts continued to live in the house until 1963, they never saw anything again.

The next occupants were a couple in their twenties, Mr and Mrs Brown. Nothing happened for another five years, until in 1968 Mr Brown was certain that they were being burgled. The intruder was a youngish man with fair hair and a pointed chin, dressed in a short coat and narrow trousers. Mr Brown woke up to find him passing by the bed, then pausing by the dressing-table as if looking for something to steal, then going across to a curtained alcove in the bedroom.

Mr Brown leaped out of bed at once, to find the "burglar" had totally vanished. He mentioned this to his uncle, a miner in his mid-fifties who had worked all his life at Askern Colliery. His uncle, Mr Holmes, refused to believe a word of it, and said that he'd stay in that room all night if necessary and prove to him there was no such thing as a ghost in there.

So Mr Holmes sat up in the room on the Browns' bed, in the dark, while his nephew and his wife stayed in the living-room downstairs. Mr Holmes was even nonchalantly smoking a cigarette. Before long he shot downstairs petrified – he had felt the side of the bed away from the door sink down as if somebody sat on it next to him! At once he had dashed over to switch on the light, only to find nobody but himself visible in the room.

That settled it – and from then on none of them ever slept in the house again, not even after the National Coal Board, who owned the house, had investigated it and found nothing apparently wrong with it.

A house in Enfield, North London, started to be haunted for no obvious reason in September, 1977. Not only did the Hodgson family, who lived there, hear someone shuffling around as if wearing badly-fitting slippers, not only did furniture move around by itself – on one occasion, after they had called in the police, a policewoman saw for herself a chair lift itself into the air, move sideways, then float back to its original position! – but the Hodgsons' nine-year-old son, Billy, narrowly escaped injury

95

when a heavy iron grate flew across him while he was lying in bed.

Worse still, one night Mrs Hodgson heard her daughter Janet, aged eleven, scream as if she were choking. She rushed into the bedroom and had to fight off a force which was wrapping a curtain round Janet's neck and choking her. Experts from Pye Electronics visited the house with some of their equipment to see if they could pick up anything, and were baffled to find that video recorders which worked perfectly well outside the house would not operate at all once they were inside.

These hauntings lasted for three years, when they came to an end just as suddenly as they had started, never to return.

And in 1981, after putting up with the disturbances which they had suffered for five months, Mr and Mrs Ralph and their baby, Charlene, had to quit their home in Sheerness, Kent. It started for no apparent reason when coins began to fly into the room, coming from somewhere near the stairs, with such force that they bounced off the floor and walls of the sitting-room. Doors would mysteriously slam shut. Light bulbs came on and went off again by themselves. And they kept hearing heavy footsteps around the house, and scraping noises, and the sound as if somebody were gasping for breath. They even called in a priest to exorcize the house, but within a few days the hauntings were back exactly as before.

One possibility was that this was caused by the ghost of Harry Morgan, who had once lived there. He had died in the house six years earlier, but it had taken several days before anyone had discovered his body. He might have been "getting his own back". Otherwise – there is no explanation which makes sense.

The House With Five Names

When Mrs Freda Kinloch came down the stairs at half-past six one evening, she saw what she thought was a nun cross the hall in front of her and go into the drawing room of the large house. It was the summer of 1882. She went into the dining room, where the rest of the family were sitting down for dinner.

"What's a nun doing in the house?" she asked. "She looks like a Sister of Mercy."

Her sister, Rosina, looked up. "I expect she's gone into the drawing room. It's only the ghost, nothing to worry about. And she's not a nun, she's just a tall lady with a handkerchief to her face. No doubt you'll be seeing her again."

Then the family got on with their dinner.

The house stands at the corner of Pitville Circus Road and All Saints Road in Cheltenham. When its first occupant, a solicitor called Henry Swinhoe, moved into the new house in 1860, he called it "Garden Reach". Later occupants renamed it first

"Pitville Hall", then "Donore", then "Inholmes", and finally "St Anne's". Its ghost became so famous that the boys of the town used to go along in the evenings to watch it cross the lawn! And apart from the boys, it was seen by at least seventeen different people and heard by more than twenty.

She might have been Henry Swinhoe's second wife. His first wife died in 1866, leaving five children, so in 1870 he married Imogen Hutchins, only to discover almost at once that she was an alcholic. She died of drink at the age of forty-one and is buried in Holy Trinity Church graveyard near her home. Henry Swinhoe himself died a year later.

The house was then bought by Benjamin Littlewood, but he died a month after he had moved in, and it stayed empty for three years. In March 1882, the Despard family moved in. There was Captain Despard and his wife, four daughters – Rosina, who was studying to become a doctor (unusual for those days), Edith aged eighteen, Lilian aged fifteen, and Mabel aged thirteen – a son, Wilfred, aged six, and another son, Henry aged sixteen, who was away at boarding school for much of the time. Mrs Freda Kinloch was a married daughter who visited her family from time to time.

Rosina saw the ghost first. She heard someone at her bedroom door one night, and when she went to look found the ghost standing outside. She saw her again about half a dozen times during the next two years. In 1883 the housemaid saw her at about ten o'clock one night, and thought that somebody had broken in. In December of the same year the figure appeared in the drawing room – Wilfred was playing outside with a friend when they both saw her through the window and raced in to find out who the lady was who was crying so much.

In January, 1884, Rosina tried to speak to the ghost. For once the ghost stopped, looked as if she were about to say something, but gave a slight gasp instead, walked off into the hall, then disappeared as she reached the side door to the house.

After that she began to be heard much more often. All the girls heard her footsteps, and so did Mrs Kinloch and the cook, as the lady passed and repassed the bedroom doors – on two different floors of the house.

Living opposite the Despards was General Annesley. On 6th August he happened to look across into the Despards' orchard. Then he sent his son across the road to ask if Mrs Kinloch was all right, and if there was anything he could do. He didn't know Mrs Kinloch by sight, since she had been staying at the house for only a few days, but thought it had to be her in the orchard, crying. It wasn't.

The ghost was seen by a number of people at various times all through that year and into 1885, especially during the summer. In fact, summer seemed to be her favourite time, because that was when the town boys always saw her. Then something extra was added, rather more sinister. A *second* set of footsteps began to be heard, walking about during much of the night every week, this time with thuds and thumps. Some of the servants promptly left, and not one of them would dare leave their rooms after they'd gone upstairs for the night.

Then something else happened. One night in July, 1886, Mrs Despard with three of her daughters and a maid all saw the flame of a candle moving about, with neither the candle itself nor any hand to hold it. At the same time there were loud noises heard coming from a room on the ground floor, and footsteps were moving up and down the stairs – with nobody there.

Captain Despard and Rosina were both away from the house that night, but when they returned and heard about this, Captain Despard at last decided that something ought to be done. He had heard that while the Swinhoes were living in the house, the second Mrs Swinhoe had dearly wanted to get her hands on the first Mrs Swinhoe's jewellery, but Henry Swinhoe had objected. What was more, he had called in a carpenter to make a box under the floorboards of one of the rooms, had placed the jewels in that and had had the boards nailed down and the carpet replaced over them.

So the Captain found the carpenter, discovered that the story was true, and called him in. The box had been placed under the floor-boards in the morning room, the very room from which the noises had been heard coming! When the carpenter took the boards up again, the box was there all right, but the jewels were now missing.

From 1887 to 1889 the appearances began to grow less frequent, although the footsteps continued to be heard. Finally they, too, faded away. The Despards moved out in 1893. For five years nobody would take the house over until it was eventually occupied by a boys' school, called "Inholmes".

Before long the apparition began to appear again – on the stairs, in the corridors, even in the boys' dormitories. When it appeared in the day-time, it always left the house and wandered down the drive. The servants left in terror and eventually the school was closed.

When the boys' school left, so did the ghost – and

began to turn up in other houses nearby instead! In 1933, for instance, Colonel Bourne and his wife, Hilda, lived at Weston House, half a mile from St Anne's, and the ghost arrived there. Hilda Bourne used to refer to the hauntings politely as "the commotion".

Their niece Jane, aged twelve, stayed with them for a while that year and saw the tall lady with a handkerchief to her face suddenly appear in the room where she was sleeping. Later, during the Second World War, a school from Birmingham was evacuated to Cheltenham and two girls of the school were accommodated by Colonel and Mrs Bourne. "The commotion" happened while they were there, but apparently they both managed to sleep through it, unlike everyone else living in the house at the time, who were all woken up. Then in 1967 Weston House became a doctors' surgery. Noises began to be heard coming from rooms on the upper floor while nobody was in them, and papers and the doctors' files rustled in rooms when they were unoccupied.

But the ghost tried other houses as well. On the opposite side of the road from St Anne's stood Cotswold Lodge. This has since been demolished, but in 1958 John Thorne, the sales manager of a brewery, had a flat there. He thought he must have been dreaming when the ghost appeared to him. But in 1961 his brother William, with his wife, son and daughter, visited him, and were persuaded to stay the night instead of going home to Maidenhead.

The flat was not very large, so William and his fifteen-year-old son had to sleep on a couch in the drawing-room. Just after midnight William heard footsteps outside the open door, and called out thinking that it must be his sister-in-law. That made his son wake up as well, and both of them found a tall woman in a long black dress with a handkerchief held to her face standing there. Then she walked off down the corridor.

Neither of them felt particularly alarmed.

"Did you see that as well?" asked his son.

"Yes. Go and close the door," said William Thorne.

His son got off the couch, went to the door, and before closing it looked up and down the corridor. It was completely empty! Neither William Thorne nor his son had ever heard of the Cheltenham ghost before, so the appearance did rather take them by surprise. It was only after they had told William's brother about it the next morning that John Thorne told them about his "dream".

Cotswold Lodge later became a hotel, and then a block of flats took its place. So far, there have been no further visitations. Perhaps the lady has just faded away . . . or perhaps has moved to somewhere else.

The Victorian Wardrobe

When Mrs Barclay visited the sale of household goods at a house near Streatley, Berkshire, she saw just what she wanted – a large Victorian wardrobe. Her own house was large, and this would suit it perfectly. The wardrobe was three metres tall and three metres wide, had four drawers, and a mirror on one of the doors. It would be just right for the guest bedroom, so she bought it, and had it delivered to her home, Carterton Manor, at Carterton, Oxfordshire. And there it remained without any bother for three years.

But then, in the spring of 1937, she and her household staff began to hear bangs and rattling noises coming from somewhere in the house, but had no idea of where it was coming from. After all, it was a large house. Perhaps it was the plumbing.

Then one by one the various guests whom she had invited to stay for weekends started to ask if there was anything strange about that old wardrobe in their room – could she explain why the doors kept opening and closing at night, by themselves, keeping them awake?

Rather surprised, she decided to keep watch herself, and found that the wardrobe doors really did seem to open and close by themselves at night. She mentioned this to a friend, Mr East, who thought that he knew what the cause might be.

"It's a Victorian wardrobe," he explained, "so there's possibly a hidden panel inside somewhere, spring-loaded. The Victorians rather went in for secret panels in wardrobes, writing desks and such, for keeping their valuables. Since the wardrobe is old, perhaps the spring keeps jumping out, knocking open the panel and causing the bother."

"But what about the noises?" she asked.

"Well, it would make a noise, wouldn't it?"

"Come and show me," said Mrs Barclay.

So they went upstairs and entered the guest bedroom. Before they had even touched the wardrobe the centre door leapt out and smashed the mirror on the opposite door!

"So it's not a hidden panel," said Mr East uneasily. "I think perhaps – er – we'd better leave it alone for a while."

And they both retreated hastily from the room.

The noises then began to be heard all over the house, growing much worse, as the wardrobe banged and rattled by itself. Then the next stage arrived. To Mrs Barclay's astonishment she saw a bent little old man in old-fashioned clothes and a deer-stalker hat came out of the wardrobe! He walked out of the room, down the stairs and out of the front door. And it was not in the dark, either, because the lights were on at the time.

This strange old man was subsequently seen by Mrs Barclay again, her secretary and brother. Each time he would be visible for half a minute, and sometimes longer, then he would vanish. Once he turned and scowled at her before walking out through the front door, banging it behind him.

Before long the ghost was becoming a serious nuisance, because in addition to the bangs and rattles from the wardrobe itself, it made such a noise as it clattered across the landing and shuffled down the stairs at all hours. The noise became, as she declared, "exasperatingly loud".

Another of Mrs Barclay's friends was a Mr E. Rundle, the landlord of the Plough Inn at Clanfield, which is only about three miles from Carterton. He suggested that what might stop it was the tying of the wardrobe doors so that they could not open. He arrived himself with a ball of thick string and tied the wardrobe up for her. In the morning, the string lay on the floor and the noises had certainly not stopped. Mrs Barclay had her bed moved out on to a flat section of the roof of the Manor House in order to be able to get some sleep! Everyone in the house saw or heard the noisy ghost.

For some reason he took a dislike to the butler, and kicked him on the leg. The maid left. Mrs Barclay's cook handed in her notice and in the meantime removed all her belongings into the village and refused to sleep in the house any longer. It was then that in desperation Mrs Barclay put an advertisement in the Personal Column of the *Morning Post* (which has since joined with the *Daily Telegraph*).

This appeared on Thursday, 19th August, 1937, and read:

For Sale – haunted wardrobe. Advertiser will be glad

to deliver same to anybody interested, complete with ghost, which would no doubt feel more at home if welcomed. Write Mrs Barclay, Carterton Manor, Oxon.

The response was astonishing. There were thirty telephone calls or telegrams that same morning. One telegram, from Chobham, Surrey, asked simply: "Can you guarantee ghost?" That one arrived just as Mrs Barclay was sitting down for lunch. Immediately she heard a noise right behind her, and turned to find the ghost standing in front of the fireplace and scowling at her before it vanished. Dozens of letters arrived by every post for the next few weeks, all either wanting to buy the wardrobe or offering well-meant advice.

The advertisement, however, was certainly a mistake, as Mrs Barclay soon discovered. The newspaper reporters arrived fairly quickly. They were followed by "ghost hunters", a great many people who were just curious and wanted to see the wardrobe for themselves, and even tourists arrived.

Mrs Barclay allowed two reporters into the house for the night, and they, her secretary and herself kept watch in the guest room, sitting in the dark. Nothing happened for an hour, then a noise started inside the large piece of furniture, "like the sound of berries falling off trees", as one reporter described it. The noise at once increased, and eventually one of the reporters shone a torch. A button mysteriously appeared on the floor in front of the wardrobe. They were convinced that something very strange was certainly happening now.

After that the practical jokers started to take part, like the one who was found running round the garden dressed in a white sheet and shouting, and others who appeared in what they thought were "ghostly" costumes and fired off pistols! And all the time the wardrobe and its ghost continued to disturb the inside of Carterton Manor with its own racket.

"We'll just have to get the thing out of the house!" exclaimed Mrs Barclay at last. So she and her secretary dragged it out into the garden, hoping that now they would be able to get some peace. Something had to be done – she must sell it as soon as possible, as she had intended!

There was one disturbing letter which arrived, which did cause Mrs Barclay to wonder whether selling it would actually solve the problem. The writer of it suggested that even if she did get rid of the wardrobe, there was no certainty that the ghost would be willing to move with it. And from what she now knew about the unpleasant little man who seemed to appear from inside it, that could have been a strong possibility.

Still, she did sell it – to Mr Rundle, of the Plough Inn at Clanfield, and he took it away. At the time, though, the Plough Inn was being rebuilt, so in the meantime he left it in an outhouse, with the intention of placing it inside his own bedroom when that was ready.

The affair now got right out of hand, because in addition to the visits by the curious and the tourists, on that first night of the wardrobe being moved, youths from miles around gathered in white sheets, shouting, throwing stones and pebbles at the roof, causing a general uproar and upsetting the whole village.

Mr Rundle, however, still thought that there had to be a logical explanation about that wardrobe. What changed his mind on that first night, in a lull in the disturbances going on outside, was when he and his wife went to the outhouse, unlocked the door and went inside. The wardrobe doors at once began to vibrate and shudder, just as they had done at Carterton Manor. It could not have been caused by anything outside, because the outhouse walls were two feet thick and made of solid Cotswold stone. Then noises began to come out of it, first curious rattlings and then "a noise like an aeroplane", according to Mrs Rundle.

After just one more night of the disturbances in the village, Mr Rundle took the wardrobe into the hotel and put it into the only room which was yet available for it.

"Somebody said they'd seen bloodstains inside it," Mrs Rundle reminded him. "Perhaps they're something to do with the cause."

"Bloodstains my foot!" grunted Mr Rundle. He knew there weren't any – that was just another of the rumours which had started. Nevertheless, it gave him an idea.

He promptly dismantled the wardrobe entirely, took it completely to pieces. There were neither bloodstains nor anything else which appear to be wrong or unusual.

So he put it back together exactly as it had been, and then they waited to see what happened. Nothing did happen, ever again. No more noises were heard coming from it, nor a bent old man seen. And from the time that the wardrobe had been removed from Carterton manor, all the disturbances there had come to an end as well, to Mrs Barclay's relief.